Travel phrasebooks collect
«Everything Will Be Okay!»

M000028970

PHRASEBOOK

— TAJIK —

By Andrey Taranov

THE MOST IMPORTANT PHRASES

This phrasebook contains
the most important
phrases and questions
for basic communication
Everything you need
to survive overseas

T&P BOOKS

Phrasebook + 3000-word dictionary

English-Tajik phrasebook & topical vocabulary

By Andrey Taranov

The collection of "Everything Will Be Okay" travel phrasebooks published by T&P Books is designed for people traveling abroad for tourism and business. The phrasebooks contain what matters most - the essentials for basic communication. This is an indispensable set of phrases to "survive" while abroad.

This book also includes a small topical vocabulary that contains roughly 3,000 of the most frequently used words. Another section of the phrasebook provides a gastronomical dictionary that may help you order food at a restaurant or buy groceries at the store.

T&P Books Publishing
www.tpbooks.com

ISBN: 978-1-78616-759-0

This book is also available in E-book formats.
Please visit www.tpbooks.com or the major online bookstores.

FOREWORD

The collection of "Everything Will Be Okay" travel phrasebooks published by T&P Books is designed for people traveling abroad for tourism and business. The phrasebooks contain what matters most - the essentials for basic communication. This is an indispensable set of phrases to "survive" while abroad.

This phrasebook will help you in most cases where you need to ask something, get directions, find out how much something costs, etc. It can also resolve difficult communication situations where gestures just won't help.

This book contains a lot of phrases that have been grouped according to the most relevant topics. The edition also includes a small vocabulary that contains roughly 3,000 of the most frequently used words. Another section of the phrasebook provides a gastronomical dictionary that may help you order food at a restaurant or buy groceries at the store.

Take "Everything Will Be Okay" phrasebook with you on the road and you'll have an irreplaceable traveling companion who will help you find your way out of any situation and teach you to not fear speaking with foreigners.

TABLE OF CONTENTS

T&P Books Publishing

PRONUNCIATION

Letter	Tajik example	T&P phonetic alphabet	English example
А а	Раҳмат!	[a]	shorter than in ask
Б б	бесоҳиб	[b]	baby, book
В в	вафодорӣ	[v]	very, river
Г г	гулмохӣ	[g]	game, gold
Ғ ғ	мурғобӣ	[ʁ]	French (guttural) R
Д д	мадд	[d]	day, doctor
Е е	телескоп	[e:]	longer than in bell
Ё ё	сайёра	[jɔ]	New York
Ж ж	аждаҳо	[ʒ]	forge, pleasure
З з	сӯзанда	[z]	zebra, please
И и	шифт	[i]	shorter than in feet
Ӣ ӣ	обчакорӣ	[i:]	feet, meter
Й й	ҳайкал	[j]	yes, New York
К к	коргардон	[k]	clock, kiss
Қ қ	нуқта	[q]	king, club
Л л	пилла	[l]	lace, people
М м	мусиқачӣ	[m]	magic, milk
Н н	нонвой	[n]	sang, thing
О о	посбон	[o:]	fall, bomb
П п	папка	[p]	pencil, private
Р р	чароғак	[r]	rice, radio
С с	суръат	[s]	city, boss
Т т	тарқиш	[t]	tourist, trip
У у	муҳаррик	[u]	book
Ӯ ӯ	кӯшк	[œ]	German Hölle
Ф ф	фурӯш	[f]	face, food
Х х	хушксолӣ	[x]	as in Scots 'loch'
Ҳ ҳ	чарогот	[h]	home, have
Ч ч	чароғ	[tʃ]	church, French
Ҷ ҷ	ҷанҷол	[dʒ]	joke, general
Ш ш	нашриёт	[ʃ]	machine, shark
Ъ ъ [1]	таърихдон	[:], [ˈ]	no sound
Э э	эҳтимолӣ	[ɛ]	man, bad
Ю ю	юнонӣ	[ju]	youth, usually
Я я	яхбурча	[ja]	Kenya, piano

Comments

[1] [:] - Lengthens the preceding vowel; ['] - after consonants is used as a 'hard sign'

LIST OF ABBREVIATIONS

English abbreviations

ab.	-	about
adj	-	adjective
adv	-	adverb
anim.	-	animate
as adj	-	attributive noun used as adjective
e.g.	-	for example
etc.	-	et cetera
fam.	-	familiar
fem.	-	feminine
form.	-	formal
inanim.	-	inanimate
masc.	-	masculine
math	-	mathematics
mil.	-	military
n	-	noun
pl	-	plural
pron.	-	pronoun
sb	-	somebody
sing.	-	singular
sth	-	something
v aux	-	auxiliary verb
vi	-	intransitive verb
vi, vt	-	intransitive, transitive verb
vt	-	transitive verb

TAJIK
PHRASEBOOK

This section contains important phrases that may come in handy in various real-life situations.
The phrasebook will help you ask for directions, clarify a price, buy tickets, and order food at a restaurant

T&P Books Publishing

PHRASEBOOK CONTENTS

T&P Books Publishing

The bare minimum

Excuse me, ... | **Бубахшед, ...**
[bubaχʃed, ...]

Hello. | **Салом.**
[salom]

Thank you. | **Ташаккур.**
[taʃakkur]

Good bye. | **То дидан.**
[to didan]

Yes. | **Ҳа.**
[ha]

No. | **Не.**
[ne]

I don't know. | **Ман намедонам.**
[man namedonam]

Where? | Where to? | When? | **Дар куҷо? | Ба куҷо? | Кай?**
[dar kuʤo? | ba kuʤo? | kaj?]

I need ... | **Ба ман ... даркор аст.**
[ba man ... darkor ast]

I want ... | **Ман ... мехоҳам.**
[man ... meχoham]

Do you have ...? | **Шумо ... доред?**
[ʃumo ... dored?]

Is there a ... here? | **Дар ин ҷо ... ҳаст?**
[dar in ʤo ... hast?]

May I ...? | **... метавонам?**
[... metavonam?]

..., please (polite request) | **Илтимос**
[iltimos]

I'm looking for ... | **Ман ... мекобам.**
[man ... mekobam]

restroom | **хоҷатхона**
[χoʤatχona]

ATM | **худпардоз**
[χudpardoz]

pharmacy (drugstore) | **дорухона**
[doruχona]

hospital | **беморхона**
[bemorχona]

police station | **идораи пулис**
[idorai pulis]

subway | **метро**
[metro]

taxi	**такси** [taksi]
train station	**вокзал** [vokzal]

My name is …	**Номи ман …** [nomi man …]
What's your name?	**Номи шумо чй?** [nomi ʃumo tʃi:?]
Could you please help me?	**Илтимос, ба ман ёрй дихед.** [iltimos, ba man jori: dihed]
I've got a problem.	**Ман мушкилй дорам.** [man muʃkili: doram]
I don't feel well.	**Худамро бад ҳис мекунам.** [χudamro bad his mekunam]
Call an ambulance!	**Ба ёрии таъҷилй занг занед!** [ba jorii ta'dʒili: zang zaned!]
May I make a call?	**Мумкин занг занам?** [mumkin zang zanam?]

I'm sorry.	**Бубахшед** [bubaχʃed]
You're welcome.	**Намеарзад** [namearzad]

I, me	**ман** [man]
you (inform.)	**ту** [tu]
he	**ӯ, вай** [œ, vaj]
she	**ӯ, вай** [œ, vaj]
they (masc.)	**онхо** [onho]
they (fem.)	**онхо** [onho]
we	**мо** [mo]
you (pl)	**шумо** [ʃumo]
you (sg, form.)	**Шумо** [ʃumo]

ENTRANCE	**ДАРОМАДГОҲ** [daromadgoh]
EXIT	**БАРОМАДГОҲ** [baromadgoh]
OUT OF ORDER	**КОР НАМЕКУНАД** [kor namekunad]
CLOSED	**ПӮШИДА** [pœʃida]

OPEN

КУШОДА
[kuʃoda]

FOR WOMEN

БАРОИ ЗАНОН
[baroi zanon]

FOR MEN

БАРОИ МАРДОН
[baroi mardon]

Questions

Where?	**Дар кучо?** [dar kudʒo?]
Where to?	**Ба кучо?** [ba kudʒo?]
Where from?	**Аз кучо?** [az kudʒo?]
Why?	**Барои чй?** [baroi tʃi:?]
For what reason?	**Чаро?** [tʃaro?]
When?	**Кай?** [kaj?]

How long?	**То кай?** [to kaj?]
At what time?	**Дар соати чанд?** [dar soati tʃand?]
How much?	**Чанд пул?** [tʃand pul?]
Do you have ...?	**Шумо ... доред?** [ʃumo ... dored?]
Where is ...?	**... дар кучо?** [... dar kudʒo?]

What time is it?	**Соат чанд?** [soat tʃand?]
May I make a call?	**Мумкин занг занам?** [mumkin zang zanam?]
Who's there?	**Кй?** [ki:?]
Can I smoke here?	**Дар ин чо сигор кашида метавонам?** [dar in dʒo sigor kaʃida metavonam?]
May I ...?	**... метавонам?** [... metavonam?]

Needs

I'd like …	**Ман … мехостам.** [man … meχostam]
I don't want …	**… намехоҳам.** [… nameχoham]
I'm thirsty.	**Ман нӯшидан мехоҳам.** [man nœʃidan meχoham]
I want to sleep.	**Ман хоб дорам.** [man χob doram]
I want …	**Ман … мехоҳам.** [man … meχoham]
to wash up	**шустушӯ кардан** [ʃustuʃœ kardan]
to brush my teeth	**дандон шустан** [dandon ʃustan]
to rest a while	**каме дам гирифтан** [kame dam giriftan]
to change my clothes	**либосамро иваз кардан** [libosamro ivaz kardan]
to go back to the hotel	**ба меҳмонхона баргаштан** [ba mehmonχona bargaʃtan]
to buy …	**… харидан** [… χaridan]
to go to …	**ба … рафтан** [ba … raftan]
to visit …	**ба … боздид кардан** [ba … bozdid kardan]
to meet with …	**вохӯрдан бо …** [voχœrdan bo …]
to make a call	**занг задан** [zang zadan]
I'm tired.	**Хаста шудам.** [χasta ʃudam]
We are tired.	**Хаста шудем.** [χasta ʃudem]
I'm cold.	**Хунук мехӯрам.** [χunuk meχœram]
I'm hot.	**Тафсидам.** [tafsidam]
I'm OK.	**Барои ман хуб.** [baroi man χub]

I need to make a call.

Ман бояд занг занам.
[man bojad zang zanam]

I need to go to the restroom.

Бояд ба хоҷатхона равам.
[bojad ba hodӡatχona ravam]

I have to go.

Бояд равам.
[bojad ravam]

I have to go now.

Ба ман рафтан лозим аст.
[ba man raftan lozim ast]

Asking for directions

Excuse me, …	**Бубахшед, …** [bubaxʃed, …]
Where is …?	**… дар кучо?** [… dar kuʤo?]
Which way is …?	**… дар кадом самт аст?** [… dar kadom samt ast?]
Could you help me, please?	**Илтимос, ба ман ёрй диҳед.** [iltimos, ba man jori: dihed]

I'm looking for …	**Ман … мекобам.** [man … mekobam]
I'm looking for the exit.	**Ман баромадгоҳ мекобам.** [man baromadgoh mekobam]
I'm going to …	**Ман ба … меравам.** [man ba … meravam]
Am I going the right way to …?	**Ман ба … дуруст меравам?** [man ba … durust meravam?]

Is it far?	**Ин дур аст?** [in dur ast?]
Can I get there on foot?	**Ба онҷо пиёда рафта метавонам?** [ba onʤo pijoda rafta metavonam?]
Can you show me on the map?	**Илтимос, дар харита нишон диҳед.** [iltimos, dar xarita niʃon dihed]
Show me where we are right now.	**Нишон диҳед, ки ҳоло мо дар кучо ҳастем.** [niʃon dihed, ki holo mo dar kuʤo hastem]

Here	**Ин ҷо** [in ʤo]
There	**Он ҷо** [on ʤo]
This way	**Ба ин ҷо** [ba in ʤo]

Turn right.	**Ба дасти рост гардед.** [ba dasti rost garded]
Turn left.	**Ба дасти чап гардед.** [ba dasti tʃap garded]
first (second, third) turn	**гардиши якум (дуюм, сеюм)** [gardiʃi jakum (dujum, sejum)]
to the right	**Ба дасти рост** [ba dasti rost]

to the left

Ба дасти чап
[ba dasti tʃap]

Go straight ahead.

Рост равед.
[rost raved]

Signs

WELCOME!	**ХУШ ОМАДЕД!** [xuʃ omaded!]
ENTRANCE	**ДАРОМАДГОҲ** [daromadgoh]
EXIT	**БАРОМАДГОҲ** [baromadgoh]

PUSH	**АЗ ХУД** [az χud]
PULL	**БА ХУД** [ba χud]
OPEN	**КУШОДА** [kuʃoda]
CLOSED	**ПӮШИДА** [pœʃida]

FOR WOMEN	**БАРОИ ЗАНОН** [baroi zanon]
FOR MEN	**БАРОИ МАРДОН** [baroi mardon]
GENTLEMEN, GENTS (m)	**ҲОҶАТХОНАИ МАРДОНА** [hodʒatχonai mardona]
WOMEN (f)	**ҲОҶАТХОНАИ ЗАНОНА** [hodʒatχonai zanona]

DISCOUNTS	**ТАХФИФ** [taχfif]
SALE	**ҲАРОҶ** [harodʒ]
FREE	**РОЙГОН** [rojgon]
NEW!	**НАВБАРОМАД!** [navbaromad!]
ATTENTION!	**ДИҚҚАТ!** [diqqat!]

NO VACANCIES	**ҶОЙ НЕСТ** [dʒoj nest]
RESERVED	**БАНД АСТ** [band ast]
ADMINISTRATION	**МАЪМУРИЯТ** [ma'murijat]
STAFF ONLY	**ТАНҲО БАРОИ ҲАЙАТ** [tanho baroi hajat]

BEWARE OF THE DOG! **САГИ ГАЗАНДА**
[sagi gazanda]

NO SMOKING! **СИГОР НАКАШЕД!**
[sigor nakaʃed!]

DO NOT TOUCH! **ЛАМС НАКУНЕД!**
[lams nakuned!]

DANGEROUS **ХАТАРНОК**
[xatarnok]

DANGER **ХАТАР**
[xatar]

HIGH VOLTAGE **ШИДДАТИ БАЛАНД**
[ʃiddati baland]

NO SWIMMING! **ОББОЗӢ МАНЪ АСТ**
[obbozi: man' ast]

OUT OF ORDER **КОР НАМЕКУНАД**
[kor namekunad]

FLAMMABLE **ОТАШАНГЕЗ**
[otaʃangez]

FORBIDDEN **МАНЪ АСТ**
[man' ast]

NO TRESPASSING! **ГУЗАШТАН МАНЪ АСТ**
[guzaʃtan man' ast]

WET PAINT **РАНГ КАРДА ШУДААСТ**
[rang karda ʃudaast]

CLOSED FOR RENOVATIONS **ПӮШИДА, ТАЪМИР МЕРАВАД**
[pœʃida, ta'mir meravad]

WORKS AHEAD **ТАЪМИРИ РОҲ**
[ta'miri roh]

DETOUR **РОҲИ ДАВРОДАВР**
[rohi davrodavr]

Transportation. General phrases

plane	**тайёра** [tajjora]
train	**қатор** [qator]
bus	**автобус** [avtobus]
ferry	**паром** [parom]
taxi	**такси** [taksi]
car	**мошин** [moʃin]

schedule	**ҷадвал** [dʒadval]
Where can I see the schedule?	**Ҷадвалро дар куҷо дидан мумкин?** [dʒadvalro dar kudʒo didan mumkin?]
workdays (weekdays)	**рӯзҳои корӣ** [rœzhoi kori:]
weekends	**рӯзҳои истироҳат** [rœzhoi istirohat]
holidays	**рӯзҳои идона** [rœzhoi idona]

DEPARTURE	**ХУРУҶ** [xurudʒ]
ARRIVAL	**ВУРУД** [vurud]
DELAYED	**ТАЪХИР ДОРАД** [ta'xir dorad]
CANCELLED	**ЛАҒВ ШУД** [laǧv ʃud]

next (train, etc.)	**навбатӣ** [navbati:]
first	**якум** [jakum]
last	**охирон** [oxiron]

When is the next ...?	**... навбатӣ кай меояд?** [... navbati: kaj meojad?]
When is the first ...?	**... якум кай меравад?** [… jakum kaj meravad?]

When is the last ...?

... охирон кай меравад?
[... oҳiron kaj meravad?]

transfer (change of trains, etc.)

гузариш
[guzariʃ]

to make a transfer

буро-фуро кардан
[buro-furo kardan]

Do I need to make a transfer?

Ба ман буро-фуро кардан лозим.
[ba man buro-furo kardan lozim]

Buying tickets

Where can I buy tickets?	**Чиптаҳоро аз кучо харида метавонам?** [tʃiptahoro az kudʒo χarida metavonam?]
ticket	**чипта** [tʃipta]
to buy a ticket	**чипта харидан** [tʃipta χaridan]
ticket price	**нархи чипта** [narχi tʃipta]
Where to?	**Ба кучо?** [ba kudʒo?]
To what station?	**То кадом истгоҳ?** [to kadom istgoh?]
I need ...	**Ба ман ... даркор аст.** [ba man ... darkor ast]
one ticket	**як чипта** [jak tʃipta]
two tickets	**ду чипта** [du tʃipta]
three tickets	**се чипта** [se tʃipta]
one-way	**ба як тараф** [ba jak taraf]
round-trip	**ба ҳар ду тараф** [ba har du taraf]
first class	**дараҷаи якум** [daradʒai jakum]
second class	**дараҷаи дуюм** [daradʒai dujum]
today	**имрӯз** [imrœz]
tomorrow	**фардо** [fardo]
the day after tomorrow	**пасфардо** [pasfardo]
in the morning	**саҳарӣ** [sahari:]
in the afternoon	**рӯзона** [rœzona]
in the evening	**бегоҳӣ** [begohi:]

aisle seat	**ҷойи назди гузаргоҳ** [dʒoji nazdi guzargoh]
window seat	**ҷойи назди тиреза** [dʒoji nazdi tireza]
How much?	**Чанд-то?** [tʃand-to?]
Can I pay by credit card?	**Бо корт пардохтан мумкин?** [bo kort pardoχtan mumkin?]

Bus

bus	**автобус** [avtobus]
intercity bus	**автобуси байнишаҳрй** [avtobusi bajniʃahri:]
bus stop	**истогоҳи автобус** [istogohi avtobus]
Where's the nearest bus stop?	**Наздиктарин истогоҳи автобус дар куҷо?** [nazdiktarin istogohi avtobus dar kudʒo?]

number (bus ~, etc.)	**рақам** [raqam]
Which bus do I take to get to …?	**Кадом автобус ба … мебарад?** [kadom avtobus ba … mebarad?]
Does this bus go to …?	**Ин автобус то … мебарад?** [in avtobus to … mebarad?]
How frequent are the buses?	**Автобусҳо зуд-зуд мегарданд?** [avtobusho zud-zud megardand?]

every 15 minutes	**ҳар понздаҳ дақиқа** [har ponzdah daqiqa]
every half hour	**ҳар ним соат** [har nim soat]
every hour	**ҳар соат** [har soat]

several times a day	**якчанд маротиба дар рӯз** [jaktʃand marotiba dar rœz]
… times a day	**… бор дар як рӯз.** [… bor dar jak rœz]

schedule	**ҷадвал** [dʒadval]
Where can I see the schedule?	**Ҷадвалро дар куҷо дидан мумкин?** [dʒadvalro dar kudʒo didan mumkin?]

When is the next bus?	**автобуси навбатй кай меояд?** [avtobusi navbati: kaj meojad?]
When is the first bus?	**автобуси якум кай меравад?** [avtobusi jakum kaj meravad?]
When is the last bus?	**автобуси охирон кай меравад?** [avtobusi oxiron kaj meravad?]

stop

истгоҳ
[istgoh]

next stop

истгоҳи оянда
[istgohi ojanda]

last stop (terminus)

истгоҳи охир
[istgohi oxir]

Stop here, please.

Лутфан, дар ҳамин ҷо нигоҳ доред.
[lutfan, dar hamin dʒo nigoh dored]

Excuse me, this is my stop.

Иҷозат диҳед, ин истгоҳи ман аст.
[idʒozat dihed, in istgohi man ast]

Train

train	**қатор** [qator]
suburban train	**қатори наздишаҳрӣ** [qatori nazdiʃahri:]
long-distance train	**қатори дуррав** [qatori durrav]
train station	**вокзал** [vokzal]
Excuse me, where is the exit to the platform?	**Бубахшед, баромадгоҳ ба назди** **қаторҳо дар куҷо?** [bubaxʃed, baromadgoh ba nazdi qatorho dar kuʤo?]
Does this train go to …?	**Ин қатор то … мебарад?** [in qator to … mebarad?]
next train	**қатори навбатӣ** [qatori navbati:]
When is the next train?	**Қатори навбатӣ кай меояд?** [qatori navbati: kaj meojad?]
Where can I see the schedule?	**Ҷадвалро дар куҷо дидан мумкин?** [ʤadvalro dar kuʤo didan mumkin?]
From which platform?	**Аз кадом платформа?** [az kadom platforma?]
When does the train arrive in …?	**Қатор ба … кай мерасад?** [qator ba … kaj merasad?]
Please help me.	**Илтимос, ба ман ёрӣ диҳед.** [iltimos, ba man jori: dihed]
I'm looking for my seat.	**Ман ҷоямро мекобам.** [man ʤojamro mekobam]
We're looking for our seats.	**Мо ҷойҳоямонро меҷӯем.** [mo ʤojhojamonro meʤœem]
My seat is taken.	**Ҷойи ман банд аст.** [ʤoji man band ast]
Our seats are taken.	**Ҷойҳои мо бананд.** [ʤojhoi mo bandand]
I'm sorry but this is my seat.	**Бубахшед, лекин ин ҷойи ман аст.** [bubaxʃed, lekin in ʤoji man ast.]
Is this seat taken?	**Ин ҷой озод аст?** [in ʤoj ozod ast?]
May I sit here?	**Ба ин ҷо шиштан мумкин?** [ba in ʤo ʃiʃtan mumkin?]

On the train. Dialogue (No ticket)

Ticket, please.
Лутфан, чиптаи шумо.
[lutfan, tʃiptai ʃumo]

I don't have a ticket.
Ман чипта надорам.
[man tʃipta nadoram]

I lost my ticket.
Ман чиптаамро гум кардам.
[man tʃiptaamro gum kardam]

I forgot my ticket at home.
Ман чиптаамро дар хона мондам.
[man tʃiptaamro dar χona mondam]

You can buy a ticket from me.
Шумо аз ман чипта харида метавонед.
[ʃumo az man tʃipta χarida metavoned]

You will also have to pay a fine.
Боз шумо бояд ҷарима супоред.
[boz ʃumo bojad dʒarima supored]

Okay.
Хуб.
[χub]

Where are you going?
Шумо ба куҷо сафар доред?
[ʃumo ba kudʒo safar dored?]

I'm going to …
Ман то … меравам.
[man to … meravam]

How much? I don't understand.
Чанд? Ман намефаҳмам.
[tʃand? man namefahmam]

Write it down, please.
Илтимос, нависед.
[iltimos, navised]

Okay. Can I pay with a credit card?
Хуб. Бо корт пардохт карда метавонам?
[χub. bo kort pardoχt karda metavonam?]

Yes, you can.
Бале, метавонед.
[bale, metavoned]

Here's your receipt.
Ана квитансияи шумо.
[ana kvitansijai ʃumo]

Sorry about the fine.
Барои ҷарима афсӯс мехӯрам.
[baroi dʒarima afsœs meχœram]

That's okay. It was my fault.
Ҳеҷ гап не. Айби худам.
[hedʒ gap ne. ajbi χudam]

Enjoy your trip.
Роҳи сафед.
[rohi safed]

Taxi

taxi	такси [taksi]
taxi driver	ронандаи такси, таксичӣ [ronandai taksi, taksitʃi:]
to catch a taxi	такси гирифтан [taksi giriftan]
taxi stand	истгоҳи такси [istgohi taksi]
Where can I get a taxi?	Дар куҷо такси ёфта метавонам? [dar kudʒo taksi jofta metavonam?]
to call a taxi	такси фармудан [taksi farmudan]
I need a taxi.	Ба ман такси даркор аст. [ba man taksi darkor ast]
Right now.	Худи ҳозир. [χudi hozir]
What is your address (location)?	Нишонии шумо? [niʃonii ʃumo?]
My address is …	Нишонии ман … [niʃonii man …]
Your destination?	Ба куҷо меравед? [ba kudʒo meraved?]
Excuse me, …	Бубахшед, … [bubaχʃed, …]
Are you available?	Шумо озод? [ʃumo ozod?]
How much is it to get to …?	То ба … чанд пул мешавад? [to ba … tʃand pul meʃavad?]
Do you know where it is?	Шумо дар куҷо буданашро медонед? [ʃumo dar kudʒo budanaʃro medoned?]
Airport, please.	Ба фурудгоҳ, хоҳиш мекунам. [ba furudgoh, χohiʃ mekunam]
Stop here, please.	Лутфан, дар ҳамин ҷо нигоҳ доред. [lutfan, dar hamin dʒo nigoh dored]
It's not here.	Дар ин ҷо не. [dar in dʒo ne]
This is the wrong address.	Ин нишонии ғалат аст. [in niʃonii ğalat ast]

Turn left.	**Ҳоло ба чап.** [holo ba tʃap]
Turn right.	**Ҳоло ба рост.** [holo ba rost]

How much do I owe you?	**Чанд пул бояд диҳам?** [tʃand pul bojad diham?]
I'd like a receipt, please.	**Лутфан, ба ман чек диҳед.** [lutfan, ba man tʃek dihed]
Keep the change.	**Бақия лозим нест.** [baqija lozim nest]

Would you please wait for me?	**Лутфан, маро мунтазир шавед.** [lutfan, maro muntazir ʃaved]
five minutes	**панҷ дақиқа** [pandʒ daqiqa]
ten minutes	**даҳ дақиқа** [dah daqiqa]
fifteen minutes	**понздаҳ дақиқа** [ponzdah daqiqa]
twenty minutes	**бист дақиқа** [bist daqiqa]
half an hour	**ним соат** [nim soat]

Hotel

Hello.	**Салом.** [salom]
My name is …	**Номи ман …** [nomi man …]
I have a reservation.	**Утоқеро резерв кардам.** [utoqero rezerv kardam]
I need …	**Ба ман … даркор аст.** [ba man … darkor ast]
a single room	**утоқи якнафара** [utoqi jaknafara]
a double room	**утоқи дунафара** [utoqi dunafara]
How much is that?	**Он чанд пул аст?** [on tʃand pul ast?]
That's a bit expensive.	**Ин каме қимат аст.** [in kame qimat ast]
Do you have anything else?	**Шумо боз ягон чизи дигар доред?** [ʃumo boz jagon tʃizi digar dored?]
I'll take it.	**Ман онро мегирам.** [man onro megiram]
I'll pay in cash.	**Ман пули нақд медиҳам.** [man puli naqd mediham]
I've got a problem.	**Ман мушкилӣ дорам.** [man muʃkili: doram]
My … is broken.	**… ман шикастагӣ.** [… man ʃikastagi:]
My … is out of order.	**… ман кор намекунад.** [… man kor namekunad]
TV	**телевизор** [televizor]
air conditioner	**кондитсионер** [konditsioner]
tap	**кран** [kran]
shower	**душ** [duʃ]
sink	**дастшӯяк** [dastʃœjak]
safe	**сейф** [sejf]

door lock	куфл [qufl]
electrical outlet	розетка [rozetka]
hairdryer	фен [fen]

I don't have …	Ман … надорам. [man … nadoram]
water	об [ob]
light	нури чароғ [nuri tʃaroğ]
electricity	барқ [barq]

Can you give me …?	Ба ман … дода метавонед? [ba man … doda metavoned?]
a towel	дастрӯймол [dastrœjmol]
a blanket	кӯрпа [kœrpa]
slippers	шиппак [ʃippak]
a robe	халат [χalat]
shampoo	шампун [ʃampun]
soap	собун [sobun]

I'd like to change rooms.	Утоқамро иваз кардан мехостам. [utoqamro ivaz kardan meχostam]
I can't find my key.	Ман калидамро ёфта наметавонам. [man kalidamro jofta nametavonam]
Could you open my room, please?	Илтимос, утоқи маро кушоед. [iltimos, utoqi maro kuʃoed]
Who's there?	Кӣ? [ki:?]
Come in!	Дароед! [daroed!]
Just a minute!	Як дақиқа! [jak daqiqa!]
Not right now, please.	Илтимос, ҳозир не. [iltimos, hozir ne]

Come to my room, please.	Марҳамат, ба утоқи ман дароед. [marhamat, ba utoqi man daroed]
I'd like to order food service.	Мехоҳам бифармоям, ки хӯрокро ба утоқам биёранд. [meχoham bifarmojam, ki χœrokro ba utoqam bijorand]

My room number is …	**Рақами утоқи ман …** [raqami utoqi man …]
I'm leaving …	**… ман аз ин ҷо меравам.** [… man az in ʤo meravam]
We're leaving …	**… мо аз ин ҷо меравем.** [… mo az in ʤo meravem]
right now	**ҳозир** [hozir]
this afternoon	**имрӯз, пас аз хӯроки нисфирӯзй** [imrœz, pas az χœroki nisfirœzi:]
tonight	**имрӯз бегоҳй** [imrœz begohi:]
tomorrow	**фардо** [fardo]
tomorrow morning	**субҳи фардо** [subhi fardo]
tomorrow evening	**шоми фардо** [ʃomi fardo]
the day after tomorrow	**пасфардо** [pasfardo]

I'd like to pay.	**Аз ман чанд пул?** [az man tʃand pul?]
Everything was wonderful.	**Ҳамааш олй буд.** [hamaaʃ oli: bud]
Where can I get a taxi?	**Дар куҷо такси ёфта метавонам?** [dar kuʤo taksi jofta metavonam?]
Would you call a taxi for me, please?	**Илтимос, ба ман такси фармоед.** [iltimos, ba man taksi farmoed]

Restaurant

Can I look at the menu, please?	**Менюи шуморо дидан мумкин?** [menjui ʃumoro didan mumkin?]
Table for one.	**Миз барои як кас.** [miz baroi jak kas]
There are two (three, four) of us.	**Мо ду (се, чор) кас.** [mo du (se, tʃor) kas]
Smoking	**Барои сигор мекашидагихо** [baroi sigor mekaʃidagiho]
No smoking	**Барои сигор намекашидагихо** [baroi sigor namekaʃidagiho]
Excuse me! (addressing a waiter)	**Лутфан!** [lutfan!]
menu	**меню, номгӯйи хӯрокхо** [menju, nomgœji χœrokho]
wine list	**корти майхо** [korti majho]
The menu, please.	**Меню, лутфан.** [menju, lutfan]
Are you ready to order?	**Шумо ба фармоиш додан омода ҳастед?** [ʃumo ba farmoiʃ dodan omoda hasted?]
What will you have?	**Чӣ мефармоед?** [tʃi: mefarmoed?]
I'll have …	**Ба ман … биёред.** [ba man … bijored]
I'm a vegetarian.	**Ман гиёҳхӯр ҳастам.** [man gijohχœr hastam]
meat	**гӯшт** [gœʃt]
fish	**моҳӣ** [mohi:]
vegetables	**сабзавот** [sabzavot]
Do you have vegetarian dishes?	**Шумо хӯрокхои бегӯшт доред?** [ʃumo χœrokhoi begœʃt dored?]
I don't eat pork.	**Ман гӯшти хук намехӯрам.** [man gœʃti χuk nameχœram]
He /she/ doesn't eat meat.	**Ӯ гӯшт намехӯрад.** [œ gœʃt nameχœrad]

I am allergic to ...

Ман ба ... ҳассосият дорам.
[man ba ... hassosijat doram]

Would you please bring me ...

Лутфан, ба ман ... биёред.
[lutfan, ba man ... bijored]

salt | pepper | sugar

намак | мурч | шакар
[namak | murtʃ | ʃakar]

coffee | tea | dessert

қаҳва | чой | ширинӣ
[qahva | tʃoj | ʃirini:]

water | sparkling | plain

об | газнок | бе газ
[ob | gaznok | be gaz]

a spoon | fork | knife

қошуқ | чангол | корд
[qoʃuq | tʃangol | kord]

a plate | napkin

табақча | дастмол
[tabaqtʃa | dastmol]

Enjoy your meal!

Иштиҳои том!
[iʃtihoi tom!]

One more, please.

Лутфан, боз биёред.
[lutfan, boz bijored]

It was very delicious.

Хеле бомаза буд.
[xele bomaza bud]

---

check | change | tip

ҳисобӣ | бақия | чойпулӣ
[hisobi: | baqija | tʃojpuli:]

Check, please.
(Could I have the check, please?)

Лутфан, ҳисоб кунед.
[lutfan, hisob kuned]

Can I pay by credit card?

Бо корт пардохта метавонам?
[bo kort pardoxta metavonam?]

I'm sorry, there's a mistake here.

Бубахшед, дар ин ҷо хато шудааст.
[bubaxʃed, dar in dʒo xato ʃudaast]

Shopping

Can I help you?
Метавонам ба шумо ёрӣ диҳам?
[metavonam ba ʃumo jori: diham?]

Do you have ...?
Шумо ... доред?
[ʃumo ... dored?]

I'm looking for ...
Ман ... мекобам.
[man ... mekobam]

I need ...
Ба ман ... даркор аст.
[ba man ... darkor ast]

I'm just looking.
Ҳамту тамошо мекунам.
[hamtu tamoʃo mekunam]

We're just looking.
Мо ҳамту тамошо мекунем
[mo hamtu tamoʃo mekunem]

I'll come back later.
Ман дертар меоям.
[man dertar meojam]

We'll come back later.
Мо дертар меоем.
[mo dertar meoem]

discounts | sale
тахфиф | ҳароҷ
[tahfif | harodʒ]

Would you please show me ...
Лутфан, ба ман ... нишон диҳед.
[lutfan, ba man ... niʃon dihed]

Would you please give me ...
Лутфан, ба ман ... диҳед.
[lutfan, ba man ... dihed]

Can I try it on?
Мумкин инро пӯшида бинам?
[mumkin inro pœʃida binam?]

Excuse me, where's the fitting room?
Ҷойи пӯшида дидан дар куҷо?
[dʒoji pœʃida didan dar kudʒo?]

Which color would you like?
Кадом рангашро мехоҳед?
[kadom rangaʃro meχohed?]

size | length
андоза | қад
[andoza | qad]

How does it fit?
Чен аст?
[tʃen ast?]

How much is it?
Ин чанд пул?
[in tʃand pul?]

That's too expensive.
Ин хеле қимат.
[in χele qimat]

I'll take it.
Ман инро мегирам.
[man inro megiram]

Excuse me, where do I pay?
Бубахшед, касса дар куҷо?
[bubaχʃed, kassa dar kudʒo?]

Will you pay in cash or credit card?	**Чй гуна пардохт мекунед?**
	Бо пули накд ё бо корт?
	[tʃi: guna pardoχt mekuned?
	bo puli naqd jo bo kort?]
In cash | with credit card	**накд | бо корт**
	[naqd | bo kort]

Do you want the receipt?	**Ба шумо чек лозим?**
	[ba ʃumo tʃek lozim?]
Yes, please.	**Бале, хоҳиш мекунам.**
	[bale, χohiʃ mekunam]
No, it's OK.	**Не, лозим нест. Ташаккур.**
	[ne, lozim nest. taʃakkur]
Thank you. Have a nice day!	**Ташаккур. Хуш бошед!**
	[taʃakkur. χuʃ boʃed!]

In town

Excuse me, please.	**Бубахшед, …** [bubaxʃed, …]
I'm looking for …	**Ман … мекобам.** [man … mekobam]
the subway	**метро** [metro]
my hotel	**меҳмонхонаамро** [mehmonxonaamro]
the movie theater	**синамо** [sinamo]
a taxi stand	**истгоҳи таски** [istgohi taski]

an ATM	**худпардоз** [xudpardoz]
a foreign exchange office	**мубодилаи асъор** [mubodilai as'or]
an internet café	**интернет-қаҳвахона** [internet-qahvaxona]
… street	**кӯчаи …** [kœtʃai …]
this place	**ана ин ҷо** [ana in dʒo]

Do you know where … is?	**Шумо медонед, ки … дар куҷо аст?** [ʃumo medoned, ki … dar kudʒo ast?]
Which street is this?	**Ин кӯча чӣ ном дорад?** [in kœtʃa tʃi: nom dorad?]
Show me where we are right now.	**Нишон диҳед, ки ҳоло мо дар куҷо ҳастем.** [niʃon dihed, ki holo mo dar kudʒo hastem]
Can I get there on foot?	**Ба онҷо пиёда рафта метавонам?** [ba ondʒo pijoda rafta metavonam?]
Do you have a map of the city?	**Шумо харитаи шаҳрро доред?** [ʃumo xaritai ʃahrro dored?]

How much is a ticket to get in?	**Чиптаи даромад чанд пул?** [tʃiptai daromad tʃand pul?]
Can I take pictures here?	**Дар ин ҷо сурат гирифтан мумкин?** [dar in dʒo surat giriftan mumkin?]
Are you open?	**Шумо кушода?** [ʃumo kuʃoda?]

When do you open?

Соати чанд кушода мешавед?
[soati tʃand kuʃoda meʃaved?]

When do you close?

То соати чанд кор мекунед?
[to soati tʃand kor mekuned?]

Money

money	**пул** [pul]
cash	**пули нақд** [puli naqd]
paper money	**пули қоғазӣ** [puli qoğazi:]
loose change	**пули майда** [puli majda]
check | change | tip	**ҳисобӣ | бақия | чойпулӣ** [hisobi: | baqija | tʃojpuli:]
credit card	**корти пластикӣ** [korti plastiki:]
wallet	**ҳамён** [hamjon]
to buy	**харид кардан** [χarid kardan]
to pay	**пардохтан** [pardoχtan]
fine	**ҷарима** [dʒarima]
free	**ройгон, бепул** [rojgon, bepul]
Where can I buy ...?	**... аз куҷо харида метавонам?** [... az kudʒo χarida metavonam?]
Is the bank open now?	**Ҳоло бонк кушода аст?** [holo bonk kuʃoda ast?]
When does it open?	**Соати чанд кушода мешавад?** [soati tʃand kuʃoda meʃavad?]
When does it close?	**То соати чанд кор мекунад?** [to soati tʃand kor mekunad?]
How much?	**Чанд?** [tʃand?]
How much is this?	**Ин чанд пул?** [in tʃand pul?]
That's too expensive.	**Ин хеле қимат.** [in χele qimat]
Excuse me, where do I pay?	**Бубахшед, касса дар куҷо?** [bubaχʃed, kassa dar kudʒo?]
Check, please.	**Лутфан, ҳисоби моро биёред.** [lutfan, hisobi moro bijored]

Can I pay by credit card?

Бо корт пардохт кардан мумкин?
[bo kort pardoχt kardan mumkin?]

Is there an ATM here?

Дар ин ҷо худпардоз ҳаст?
[dar in dʒo χudpardoz hast?]

I'm looking for an ATM.

Ба ман худпардоз лозим аст.
[ba man χudpardoz lozim ast]

I'm looking for a foreign exchange office.

Ман саррофӣ мекобам.
[man sarrofi: mekobam]

I'd like to change …

… иваз кардан мехостам.
[… ivaz kardan meχostam]

What is the exchange rate?

Нархи арз чи қадр аст?
[narχi arz tʃi qadr ast?]

Do you need my passport?

Ба шумо шиносномаи ман даркор?
[ba ʃumo ʃinosnomai man darkor?]

Time

What time is it?	**Соат чанд?** [soat tʃand?]
When?	**Кай?** [kaj?]
At what time?	**Соати чанд?** [soati tʃand?]
now | later | after …	**хозир | дертар | баъди …** [hozir | dertar | ba'di …]
one o'clock	**яки рӯз** [jaki rœz]
one fifteen	**яку понздаҳ** [jaku ponzdah]
one thirty	**яку ним** [jaku nim]
one forty-five	**понздаҳто кам ду** [ponzdahto kam du]
one | two | three	**як | ду | се** [jak | du | se]
four | five | six	**чор | панҷ | шаш** [tʃor | pandʒ | ʃaʃ]
seven | eight | nine	**ҳафт | ҳашт | нӯҳ** [haft | haʃt | nœh]
ten | eleven | twelve	**даҳ | ёздаҳ | дувоздаҳ** [dah | jozdah | duvozdah]
in …	**баъди …** [ba'di …]
five minutes	**панҷ дақиқа** [pandʒ daqiqa]
ten minutes	**даҳ дақиқа** [dah daqiqa]
fifteen minutes	**понздаҳ дақиқа** [ponzdah daqiqa]
twenty minutes	**бист дақиқа** [bist daqiqa]
half an hour	**ним соат** [nim soat]
an hour	**як соат** [jak soat]
in the morning	**саҳарӣ** [sahari:]
early in the morning	**саҳари барвақт** [sahari barvaqt]

this morning	**имрӯз саҳарӣ** [imrœz sahari:]
tomorrow morning	**субҳи фардо** [subhi fardo]

in the middle of the day	**дар нисфирӯзӣ** [dar nisfirœzi:]
in the afternoon	**баъди нисфирӯзӣ** [ba'di nisfirœzi:]
in the evening	**бегоҳӣ** [begohi:]
tonight	**имрӯз бегоҳӣ** [imrœz begohi:]

at night	**шабона** [ʃabona]
yesterday	**дирӯз** [dirœz]
today	**имрӯз** [imrœz]
tomorrow	**пагоҳ** [pagoh]
the day after tomorrow	**пасфардо** [pasfardo]

What day is it today?	**Имрӯз кадом рӯз аст?** [imrœz kadom rœz ast?]
It's …	**Имрӯз …** [imrœz …]
Monday	**душанбе** [duʃanbe]
Tuesday	**сешанбе** [seʃanbe]
Wednesday	**чоршанбе** [tʃorʃanbe]

Thursday	**панҷшанбе** [pandʒʃanbe]
Friday	**ҷумъа** [dʒum'a]
Saturday	**шанбе** [ʃanbe]
Sunday	**якшанбе** [jakʃanbe]

Greetings. Introductions

Hello.	**Салом.** [salom]
Pleased to meet you.	**Аз шиносой бо шумо хурсандам.** [az ʃinosoi: bo ʃumo χursandam]
Me too.	**Ман ҳам.** [man ham]
I'd like you to meet …	**Шинос шавед. Ин кас …** [ʃinos ʃaved. in kas …]
Nice to meet you.	**Аз ошной бо шумо шод шудам.** [az oʃnoi: bo ʃumo ʃod ʃudam]

How are you?	**Шумо чй хел? Корхоятон чй хел?** [ʃumo tʃi? χel? korhojaton tʃi: χel?]
My name is …	**Номи ман …** [nomi man …]
His name is …	**Номи вай …** [nomi vaj …]
Her name is …	**Номи вай …** [nomi vaj …]

What's your name?	**Номи шумо чй?** [nomi ʃumo tʃi:?]
What's his name?	**Номи вай чй?** [nomi vaj tʃi:?]
What's her name?	**Номи вай чй?** [nomi vaj tʃi:?]

What's your last name?	**Насаби шумо чй?** [nasabi ʃumo tʃi:?]
You can call me …	**Маро … ном гиред.** [maro … nom gired]
Where are you from?	**Шумо аз куҷо?** [ʃumo az kudʒo?]
I'm from …	**Ман аз …** [man az …]
What do you do for a living?	**Кй шуда кор мекунед?** [ki: ʃuda kor mekuned?]

Who is this?	**Ин кй?** [in ki:?]
Who is he?	**Вай кй?** [vaj ki:?]
Who is she?	**Вай кй?** [vaj ki:?]

Who are they?	**Онҳо кӣ?** [onho ki:?]
This is …	**Ин кас …** [in kas …]
my friend (masc.)	**дӯсти ман** [dœsti man]
my friend (fem.)	**дугонаи ман** [dugonai man]
my husband	**шавҳари ман** [ʃavhari man]
my wife	**завҷаи ман** [zavdʒai man]
my father	**падари ман** [padari man]
my mother	**модари ман** [modari man]
my brother	**бародари ман** [barodari man]
my sister	**хоҳари ман** [χohari man]
my son	**писари ман** [pisari man]
my daughter	**духтари ман** [duχtari man]
This is our son.	**Ин писари мо.** [in pisari mo]
This is our daughter.	**Ин духтари мо.** [in duχtari mo]
These are my children.	**Инҳо фарзандони ман.** [inho farzandoni man]
These are our children.	**Инҳо фарзандони мо.** [inho farzandoni mo]

Farewells

Good bye!
То дидан!
[to didan!]

Bye! (inform.)
Хайр!
[χajr!]

See you tomorrow.
То пагоҳ.
[to pagoh]

See you soon.
То боздид.
[to bozdid]

See you at seven.
Соати ҳафт вомехӯрем.
[soati haft vomeχœrem]

Have fun!
Вақтхушй кунед!
[vaqtχuʃi: kuned!]

Talk to you later.
Дертар гап мезанем.
[dertar gap mezanem]

Have a nice weekend.
Рӯзҳои истироҳатро хуб гузаронед.
[rœzhoi istirohatro χub guzaroned]

Good night.
Шаби хуш.
[ʃabi χuʃ]

It's time for me to go.
Бояд равам.
[bojad ravam]

I have to go.
Бояд равам.
[bojad ravam]

I will be right back.
Ман ҳозир бармегардам.
[man hozir barmegardam]

It's late.
Хеле бевақт шуд.
[χele bevaqt ʃud]

I have to get up early.
Пагоҳ бояд барвақт хезам.
[pagoh bojad barvaqt χezam]

I'm leaving tomorrow.
Пагоҳ ман меравам.
[pagoh man meravam]

We're leaving tomorrow.
Пагоҳ мо меравем.
[pagoh mo meravem]

Have a nice trip!
Роҳи сафед!
[rohi safed!]

It was nice meeting you.
Хурсандам, ки бо шумо шинос шудам.
[χursandam, ki bo ʃumo ʃinos ʃudam]

It was nice talking to you.
Аз суҳбати шумо баҳра бурдам.
[az suhbati ʃumo bahra burdam]

Thanks for everything.	**Ташаккур барои ҳама чиз.** [taʃakkur baroi hama tʃiz]
I had a very good time.	**Вақтам хеле хуб гузашт.** [vaqtam χele χub guzaʃt]
We had a very good time.	**Вақтамон хеле хуб гузашт.** [vaqtamon χele χub guzaʃt]
It was really great.	**Ҳама чиз олӣ буд.** [hama tʃiz oli: bud]
I'm going to miss you.	**Ёд мекунам.** [jod mekunam]
We're going to miss you.	**Мо ёд мекунем.** [mo jod mekunem]

Good luck!	**Комрон бош! Хайр!** [komron boʃ! χajr!]
Say hi to …	**Ба ... салом расонед.** [ba ... salom rasoned]

Foreign language

I don't understand.	**Ман намефаҳмам.** [man namefahmam]
Write it down, please.	**Лутфан, инро бинависед.** [lutfan, inro binavised]
Do you speak …?	**Шумо забони … медонед?** [ʃumo zaboni … medoned?]

I speak a little bit of …	**Каме … медонам** [kame … medonam]
English	**инглисӣ** [inglisi:]
Turkish	**туркӣ** [turki:]
Arabic	**арабӣ** [arabi:]
French	**фаронсавӣ** [faronsavi:]

German	**олмонӣ** [olmoni:]
Italian	**итолиёӣ** [itolijoi:]
Spanish	**испанӣ** [ispani:]
Portuguese	**португалӣ** [portugali:]
Chinese	**чинӣ** [tʃini:]
Japanese	**ҷопонӣ** [dʒoponi:]

Can you repeat that, please.	**Лутфан, такрор кунед.** [lutfan, takror kuned]
I understand.	**Мефаҳмам.** [mefahmam]
I don't understand.	**Ман намефаҳмам.** [man namefahmam]
Please speak more slowly.	**Лутфан, оҳиста гап занед.** [lutfan, ohista gap zaned]

Is that correct? (Am I saying it right?)	**Ин дуруст?** [in durust?]
What is this? (What does this mean?)	**Ин калима чӣ маъно дорад?** [in kalima tʃi: ma'no dorad?]

Apologies

Excuse me, please.	**Илтимос, бубахшед.** [iltimos, bubaxʃed]
I'm sorry.	**Афсӯс мехӯрам.** [afsœs meχœram]
I'm really sorry.	**Сад афсӯс.** [sad afsœs]
Sorry, it's my fault.	**Айби ман шуд.** [ajbi man ʃud]
My mistake.	**Хатои ман.** [χatoi man]
May I ...?	**Мумкин ман...** [mumkin man ...]
Do you mind if I ...?	**Агар зид набошед, ман ...** [agar zid naboʃed, man ...]
It's OK.	**Ҳеҷ гап не.** [heʤ gap ne]
It's all right.	**Ҳамааш дар ҷояш.** [hamaaʃ dar ʤojaʃ]
Don't worry about it.	**Ташвиш накашед.** [taʃviʃ nakaʃed]

Agreement

Yes.	**Ҳа.** [ha]
Yes, sure.	**Ҳа, албатта.** [ha, albatta]
OK (Good!)	**Хуб!** [χub!]
Very well.	**Хеле хуб!** [χele χub!]
Certainly!	**Албатта!** [albatta!]
I agree.	**Ман розй** [man rozi:]
That's correct.	**Рост.** [rost]
That's right.	**Дуруст.** [durust]
You're right.	**Шумо ҳақ.** [ʃumo haq]
I don't mind.	**Эътироз намекунам.** [e'tiroz namekunam]
Absolutely right.	**Комилан дуруст.** [komilan durust]
It's possible.	**Ин инконпазир аст.** [in inkonpazir ast]
That's a good idea.	**Ин фикри хуб.** [in fikri χub]
I can't say no.	**Не гуфта наметавонам.** [ne gufta nametavonam]
I'd be happy to.	**Хурсанд мешавам.** [χursand meʃavam]
With pleasure.	**Бо камоли майл.** [bo kamoli majl]

Refusal. Expressing doubt

No.
Не.
[ne]

Certainly not.
Албатта не.
[albatta ne]

I don't agree.
Ман розӣ не.
[man rozi: ne]

I don't think so.
Фикри ман дигар.
[fikri man digar]

It's not true.
Ин рост не.
[in rost ne]

You are wrong.
Шумо ҳақ нестед.
[ʃumo haq nested]

I think you are wrong.
Ба фикрам, ҳақ бар ҷониби шумо нест.
[ba fikram, haq bar dʒonibi ʃumo nest]

I'm not sure.
Дилпур нестам.
[dilpur nestam]

It's impossible.
Ин аз имкон берун аст.
[in az imkon berun ast]

Nothing of the kind (sort)!
Асло!
[aslo!]

The exact opposite.
Баръакс!
[bar'aks!]

I'm against it.
Ман зид.
[man zid]

I don't care.
Ба ман фарқ надорад.
[ba man farq nadorad]

I have no idea.
Хабар надорам.
[χabar nadoram]

I doubt it.
Аз ин шубҳа дорам.
[az in ʃubha doram]

Sorry, I can't.
Бубахшед, ман наметавонам.
[bubaχʃed, man nametavonam]

Sorry, I don't want to.
Бубахшед, ман намехоҳам.
[bubaχʃed, man nameχoham]

Thank you, but I don't need this.
Ташаккур, ин ба ман даркор не.
[taʃakkur, in ba man darkor ne]

It's getting late.
Хеле бевақт шуд.
[χele bevaqt ʃud]

I have to get up early.

Пагоҳ бояд барвақт хезам.
[pagoh bojad barvaqt χezam]

I don't feel well.

Худамро бад ҳис мекунам.
[χudamro bad his mekunam]

Expressing gratitude

Thank you.
Ташаккур.
[taʃakkur]

Thank you very much.
Ташаккури зиёд.
[taʃakkuri zijod]

I really appreciate it.
Сипосгузорам.
[siposguzoram]

I'm really grateful to you.
Аз шумо миннатдорам.
[az ʃumo minnatdoram]

We are really grateful to you.
Аз шумо сипосгузорем.
[az ʃumo siposguzorem]

Thank you for your time.
Ташаккур, ки вақт сарф кардед.
[taʃakkur, ki vaqt sarf karded.]

Thanks for everything.
Ташаккур барои ҳама чиз.
[taʃakkur baroi hama tʃiz]

Thank you for ...
Ташаккур барои ...
[taʃakkur baroi ...]

your help
ёрии шумо
[jorii ʃumo]

a nice time
вақти хуш
[vaqti χuʃ]

a wonderful meal
хӯроки бомаза
[χœroki bomaza]

a pleasant evening
шоми хуш
[ʃomi χuʃ]

a wonderful day
рӯзи хотирмон
[rœzi χotirmon]

an amazing journey
экскурсияи шавқовар
[ekskursijai ʃavqovar]

Don't mention it.
Ҳеҷ гап не.
[heʤ gap ne]

You are welcome.
Намеарзад.
[namearzad]

Any time.
Ҳамеша марҳамат.
[hameʃa marhamat]

My pleasure.
Хушҳолам, ки кӯмак кардам.
[χuʃholam, ki kœmak kardam]

Forget it.
Фаромӯш кунед. Ҳамааш дар ҷояш.
[faromœʃ kuned. hamaaʃ dar ʤojaʃ]

Don't worry about it.
Ташвиш накашед.
[taʃviʃ nakaʃed]

Congratulations. Best wishes

Congratulations!	**Табрик мекунам!** [tabrik mekunam!]
Happy birthday!	**Зодрӯз муборак!** [zodrœz muborak!]
Merry Christmas!	**Иди милод муборак!** [idi milod muborak!]
Happy New Year!	**Соли нав муборак!** [soli nav muborak!]
Happy Easter!	**Иди Песоҳ муборак!** [idi pesoh muborak!]
Happy Hanukkah!	**Иди Ханука муборак!** [idi χanuka muborak!]
I'd like to propose a toast.	**Нӯшбод дорам.** [nœʃbod doram]
Cheers!	**Барои саломатии шумо!** [baroi salomatii ʃumo!]
Let's drink to …!	**Барои ... менӯшем!** [baroi ... menœʃem!]
To our success!	**Барои комёбии мо!** [baroi komjobii mo!]
To your success!	**Барои комёбии шумо!** [baroi komjobii ʃumo!]
Good luck!	**Муваффақият!** [muvaffaqijat!]
Have a nice day!	**Рӯзи хуш!** [rœzi χuʃ!]
Have a good holiday!	**Хуб дам гиред!** [χub dam gired!]
Have a safe journey!	**Сафари хуш бод!** [safari χuʃ bod!]
I hope you get better soon!	**Орзу мекунам, ки зудтар сиҳат шавед!** [orzu mekunam, ki zudtar sihat ʃaved!]

Socializing

Why are you sad?	**Чаро озурда менамоед?** [tʃaro ozurda menamoed?]
Smile! Cheer up!	**Табассум кунед!** [tabassum kuned!]
Are you free tonight?	**Бегоҳӣ кор надоред?** [begohi: kor nadored?]
May I offer you a drink?	**Мумкин ба шумо нӯшокӣ пешкаш кунам?** [mumkin ba ʃumo nœʃoki: peʃkaʃ kunam?]
Would you like to dance?	**Рақс кардан намехоҳед?** [raqs kardan nameχohed?]
Let's go to the movies.	**Шояд ба синамо равем?** [ʃojad ba sinamo ravem?]
May I invite you to …?	**Мумкин шуморо ба … таклиф кунам?** [mumkin ʃumoro ba … taklif kunam?]
a restaurant	**тарабхона** [tarabχona]
the movies	**синамо** [sinamo]
the theater	**театр** [teatr]
go for a walk	**сайру гашт** [sajru gaʃt]
At what time?	**Соати чанд?** [soati tʃand?]
tonight	**имрӯз бегоҳӣ** [imrœz begohi:]
at six	**дар соати шаш** [dar soati ʃaʃ]
at seven	**дар соати ҳафт** [dar soati haft]
at eight	**дар соати ҳашт** [dar soati haʃt]
at nine	**дар соати нуҳ** [dar soati nuh]
Do you like it here?	**Ба шумо ин ҷо маъқул?** [ba ʃumo in dʒo ma'qul?]
Are you here with someone?	**Шумо дар ин ҷо танҳо?** [ʃumo dar in dʒo tanho?]

I'm with my friend.

Ман бо дӯстам /дугонаам/.
[man bo dœstam /dugonaam/]

I'm with my friends.

Ман бо дӯстонам.
[man bo dœstonam]

No, I'm alone.

Ман танхо.
[man tanho]

Do you have a boyfriend?

Ту рафиқ дорй?
[tu rafiq dori:?]

I have a boyfriend.

Ман чӯра дорам.
[man dʒœra doram]

Do you have a girlfriend?

Ту дугона дорй?
[tu dugona dori:?]

I have a girlfriend.

Ман хонум дорам.
[man χonum doram]

Can I see you again?

Боз вомехӯрем?
[boz vomeχœrem?]

Can I call you?

Мумкин ба ту занг занам?
[mumkin ba tu zang zanam?]

Call me. (Give me a call.)

Ба ман занг зан.
[ba man zang zan]

What's your number?

Рақмат чанд?
[raqmat tʃand?]

I miss you.

Туро ёд мекунам.
[turo jod mekunam]

You have a beautiful name.

Номатон бисёр зебо.
[nomaton bisjor zebo]

I love you.

Ман туро дӯст медорам.
[man turo dœst medoram]

Will you marry me?

Ҳамсари ман шав.
[hamsari man ʃav]

You're kidding!

Шӯхй мекунед!
[ʃœχi: mekuned!]

I'm just kidding.

Ҳамту шӯхй буд.
[hamtu ʃœχi: bud]

Are you serious?

Шумо чиддй мегӯед?
[ʃumo dʒiddi: megœed?]

I'm serious.

Ман чиддй мегӯям.
[man dʒiddi: megœjam]

Really?!

Рост?!
[rost?!]

It's unbelievable!

Ин аз ақл берун!
[in az aql berun!]

I don't believe you.

Ман ба шумо бовар намекунам.
[man ba ʃumo bovar namekunam]

I can't.

Ман наметавонам.
[man nametavonam]

I don't know.

Ман намедонам.
[man namedonam]

I don't understand you.	**Ман шуморо намефаҳмам.** [man ʃumoro namefahmam]
Please go away.	**Лутафан, биравед.** [lutafan, biraved]
Leave me alone!	**Маро ташвиш надиҳед!** [maro taʃviʃ nadihed!]

I can't stand him.	**Ман вайро тоқати дидан надорам.** [man vajro toqati didan nadoram]
You are disgusting!	**Шумо нафратангез!** [ʃumo nafratangez!]
I'll call the police!	**Ман ба пулис занг мезанам!** [man ba pulis zang mezanam!]

Sharing impressions. Emotions

I like it.	**Ин ба ман маъқул.**
	[in ba man ma'qul]
Very nice.	**Хеле дилкаш.**
	[χele dilkaʃ]
That's great!	**Ин зӯр!**
	[in zœr!]
It's not bad.	**Ин бад не.**
	[in bad ne]

I don't like it.	**Ин ба ман маъқул не.**
	[in ba man ma'qul ne]
It's not good.	**Ин хуб не.**
	[in χub ne]
It's bad.	**Ин бад.**
	[in bad]
It's very bad.	**Ин хеле бад.**
	[in χele bad]
It's disgusting.	**Ин нафратангез.**
	[in nafratangez]

I'm happy.	**Ман хушбахт.**
	[man χuʃbaχt]
I'm content.	**Ман қаноатманд.**
	[man qanoatmand]
I'm in love.	**Ман ошиқ шудам.**
	[man oʃiq ʃudam]
I'm calm.	**Ман ором.**
	[man orom]
I'm bored.	**Дилгир шудам.**
	[dilgir ʃudam]

I'm tired.	**Монда шудам.**
	[monda ʃudam]
I'm sad.	**Зиқ шудам.**
	[ziq ʃudam]
I'm frightened.	**Ман метарсам.**
	[man metarsam]

I'm angry.	**Қаҳрам меояд.**
	[qahram meojad]
I'm worried.	**Ман дар ҳаяҷонам.**
	[man dar hajadʒonam]
I'm nervous.	**Асабонӣ мешавам.**
	[asaboni: meʃavam]

I'm jealous. (envious)

Ман ҳасад мебарам.
[man hasad mebaram]

I'm surprised.

Ман ҳайрон.
[man hajron]

I'm perplexed.

Дар тааччубам.
[dar taadʒdʒubam]

Problems. Accidents

I've got a problem.	**Ман мушкилӣ дорам.** [man muʃkili: doram]
We've got a problem.	**Мо мушкилӣ дорем.** [mo muʃkili: dorem]
I'm lost.	**Ман раҳгум задам.** [man rahgum zadam]
I missed the last bus (train).	**Ман ба автобуси (қатори) охирон дер кардам.** [man ba avtobusi (qatori) oxiron der kardam]
I don't have any money left.	**Ман тамоман бепул мондам.** [man tamoman bepul mondam]

I've lost my ...	**Ман ... гум кардам.** [man ... gum kardam]
Someone stole my ...	**... дуздиданд.** [... duzdidand]

passport	**шиносномаамро** [ʃinosnomaamro]
wallet	**ҳамёнамро** [hamjonamro]
papers	**ҳуҷҷатҳоямро** [huʤʤathojamro]
ticket	**чиптаамро** [tʃiptaamro]

money	**пулҳоямро** [pulhojamro]
handbag	**сумкаамро** [sumkaamro]
camera	**суратгиракамро** [suratgirakamro]
laptop	**ноутбукамро** [noutbukamro]
tablet computer	**планшетамро** [planʃetamro]
mobile phone	**телефонамро** [telefonamro]

Help me!	**Ёрӣ диҳед!** [jori: dihed!]
What's happened?	**Чӣ шуд?** [tʃi: ʃud?]

fire	**сӯхтор** [sœχtor]
shooting	**тирпаронй** [tirparoni:]
murder	**куштор** [kuʃtor]
explosion	**таркиш** [tarkiʃ]
fight	**занозанй** [zanozani:]

Call the police!	**Ба пулис занг занед!** [ba pulis zang zaned!]
Please hurry up!	**Илтимос, зудтар!** [iltimos, zudtar!]
I'm looking for the police station.	**Ман идораи пулис мекобам.** [man idorai pulis mekobam.]
I need to make a call.	**Ба занг задан даркор.** [ba zang zadan darkor]
May I use your phone?	**Мумкин занг занам?** [mumkin zang zanam?]

I've been ...	**Маро** [maro]
mugged	**ғорат карданд** [ǧorat kardand]
robbed	**дузд зад** [duzd zad]
raped	**таҷовуз кардан** [tadʒovuz kardan]
attacked (beaten up)	**лату кӯб карданд** [latu kœb kardand]

Are you all right?	**Ҳолатон хуб?** [holaton χub?]
Did you see who it was?	**Шумо дидед, вай кй буд?** [ʃumo dided, vaj ki: bud?]
Would you be able to recognize the person?	**Вайро шинохта метавонед?** [vajro ʃinoχta metavoned?]
Are you sure?	**Шумо аниқ медонед?** [ʃumo aniq medoned?]

Please calm down.	**Илтимос, ором шавед.** [iltimos, orom ʃaved]
Take it easy!	**Ором!** [orom!]
Don't worry!	**Ташвиш накашед.** [taʃviʃ nakaʃed]
Everything will be fine.	**Ҳамааш хуб мешавад.** [hamaaʃ χub meʃavad]
Everything's all right.	**Ҳамааш дар ҷояш.** [hamaaʃ dar dʒojaʃ]

Come here, please.

Лутфан, наздик оед.
[lutfan, nazdik oed]

I have some questions for you.

Ба шумо якчанд савол дорам.
[ba ʃumo jaktʃand savol doram]

Wait a moment, please.

Лутфан, мунтазир шавед.
[lutfan, muntazir ʃaved]

Do you have any I.D.?

Шумо ҳуҷҷат доред?
[ʃumo huʤʤat dored?]

Thanks. You can leave now.

Ташаккур. Шумо рафта метавонед.
[taʃakkur. ʃumo rafta metavoned]

Hands behind your head!

Дастҳо пушти сар!
[dastho puʃti sar!]

You're under arrest!

Шумо ҳабс шудед!
[ʃumo habs ʃuded!]

Health problems

Please help me.	**Лутфан, ёрй диҳед.** [lutfan, jori: dihed]
I don't feel well.	**Худамро бад ҳис мекунам.** [χudamro bad his mekunam]
My husband doesn't feel well.	**Ҳоли шавҳарам бад шуд.** [holi ʃavharam bad ʃud]
My son …	**Ҳоли писарам …** [holi pisaram …]
My father …	**Ҳоли падарам …** [holi padaram …]
My wife doesn't feel well.	**Ҳоли занам бад шуд.** [holi zanam bad ʃud]
My daughter …	**Ҳоли духтарам …** [holi duχtaram …]
My mother …	**Ҳоли модарам …** [holi modaram …]
I've got a …	**… дард мекунад.** [… dard mekunad]
headache	**сарам** [saram]
sore throat	**гулӯям** [gulœjam]
stomach ache	**шикамам** [ʃikamam]
toothache	**дандонам** [dandonam]
I feel dizzy.	**Сарам тоб мехӯрад.** [saram tob meχœrad]
He has a fever.	**Тафс дорам.** [tafs doram]
She has a fever.	**Вай тафс дорад.** [vaj tafs dorad]
I can't breathe.	**Нафас кашида наметавонам.** [nafas kaʃida nametavonam]
I'm short of breath.	**Нафасгир мешавам.** [nafasgir meʃavam]
I am asthmatic.	**Ман астма дорам.** [man astma doram]
I am diabetic.	**Ман қандкасалам.** [man qandkasalam]

I can't sleep. **Бедорхобӣ мекашам.**
[bedorχobi: mekaʃam]

food poisoning **Захролудшавии ғизой**
[zahroludʃavii ǧizoi:]

It hurts here. **Ин ҷоям дард мекунад.**
[in dӡojam dard mekunad]

Help me! **Ёрӣ диҳед!**
[jori: dihed!]

I am here! **Ман ҳамин ҷо!**
[man hamin dӡo!]

We are here! **Мо ҳамин ҷо!**
[mo hamin dӡo!]

Get me out of here! **Маро кашида баroutеред!**
[maro kaʃida barored!]

I need a doctor. **Ба ман духтур даркор.**
[ba man duχtur darkor]

I can't move. **Ҳаракат карда наметавонам.**
[harakat karda nametavonam]

I can't move my legs. **Пойҳоямро ҳис намекунам.**
[pojhojamro his namekunam]

I have a wound. **Ман захм хӯрдам.**
[man zaχm χœrdam]

Is it serious? **Ин ҷиддӣ?**
[in dӡiddi:?]

My documents are in my pocket. **Ҳуҷҷатҳоям дар киса.**
[hudӡdӡathojam dar kisa]

Calm down! **Ором шавед!**
[orom ʃaved!]

May I use your phone? **Мумкин занг занам?**
[mumkin zang zanam?]

Call an ambulance! **Ба ёрии таъҷилӣ занг занед!**
[ba jorii ta'dӡili: zang zaned!]

It's urgent! **Ин фаврӣ!**
[in favri:!]

It's an emergency! **Ин бисёр фаврӣ!**
[in bisjor favri:!]

Please hurry up! **Илтимос, зудтар!**
[iltimos, zudtar!]

Would you please call a doctor? **Илтимос, духтурро чеғ занед.**
[iltimos, duχturro dӡeǧ zaned]

Where is the hospital? **Беморохона дар куҷо?**
[bemoroχona dar kudӡo?]

How are you feeling? **Худро чи хел ҳис мекунед?**
[χudro tʃi χel his mekuned?]

Are you all right? **Ҳолатон хуб?**
[holaton χub?]

What's happened? **Чӣ рӯй дод?**
[tʃi: rœj dod?]

I feel better now.	**Аллакай, худро беҳтар ҳис мекунам.** [allakaj, χudro behtar his mekunam]
It's OK.	**Ҳамааш дар ҷояш.** [hamaaʃ dar ʤojaʃ]
It's all right.	**Ҳамааш хуб.** [hamaaʃ χub]

At the pharmacy

pharmacy (drugstore)	дорухона [doruχona]
24-hour pharmacy	дорухонаи шабонарӯзӣ [doruχonai ʃabonarœzi:]
Where is the closest pharmacy?	Дорухонаи наздиктарин дар кучо? [doruχonai nazdiktarin dar kudʒo?]

Is it open now?	Холо кушода аст? [holo kuʃoda ast?]
At what time does it open?	Соати чанд кушода мешавад? [soati tʃand kuʃoda meʃavad?]
At what time does it close?	То соати чанд кор мекунад? [to soati tʃand kor mekunad?]

Is it far?	Ин дур аст? [in dur ast?]
Can I get there on foot?	Ба онҷо пиёда рафта метавонам? [ba ondʒo pijoda rafta metavonam?]
Can you show me on the map?	Илтимос, дар харита нишон диҳед. [iltimos, dar χarita niʃon dihed]

Please give me something for ...	Ба ман ягон чиз аз ... диҳед. [ba man jagon tʃiz az ... dihed]
a headache	дарди сар [dardi sar]
a cough	сулфа [sulfa]
a cold	шамолхӯрӣ [ʃamolχœri:]
the flu	зуком [zukom]

a fever	тафс [tafs]
a stomach ache	дарди меъда [dardi me'da]
nausea	дилбехузурӣ [dilbehuzuri:]
diarrhea	шикамравӣ [ʃikamravi:]
constipation	қабзият [qabzijat]
pain in the back	дарди миён [dardi mijon]

chest pain	**дарди қафаси сина** [dardi qafasi sina]
side stitch	**дарди паҳлӯ** [dardi pahlœ]
abdominal pain	**дарди шикам** [dardi ʃikam]

pill	**доруи ҳаб** [dorui hab]
ointment, cream	**марҳам, крем** [marham, krem]
syrup	**шира** [ʃira]
spray	**спрей** [sprej]
drops	**чакрагӣ** [tʃakragi:]

You need to go to the hospital.	**Шумо бояд ба беморхона равед.** [ʃumo bojad ba bemorχona raved]
health insurance	**таъминот** [ta'minot]
prescription	**ретсепт** [retsept]
insect repellant	**доруи ҳашарот** [dorui haʃarot]
Band Aid	**часпи захм** [tʃaspi zaχm]

The bare minimum

Excuse me, …	**Бубахшед, …** [bubaχʃed, …]
Hello.	**Салом.** [salom]
Thank you.	**Ташаккур.** [taʃakkur]
Good bye.	**То дидан.** [to didan]
Yes.	**Ҳа.** [ha]
No.	**Не.** [ne]
I don't know.	**Ман намедонам.** [man namedonam]
Where? | Where to? | When?	**Дар куҷо? | Ба куҷо? | Кай?** [dar kuʤo? | ba kuʤo? | kaj?]

I need …	**Ба ман … даркор аст.** [ba man … darkor ast]
I want …	**Ман … мехоҳам.** [man … meχoham]
Do you have …?	**Шумо … доред?** [ʃumo … dored?]
Is there a … here?	**Дар ин ҷо … ҳаст?** [dar in ʤo … hast?]
May I …?	**… метавонам?** [… metavonam?]
…, please (polite request)	**Илтимос** [iltimos]

I'm looking for …	**Ман … мекобам.** [man … mekobam]
restroom	**хоҷатхона** [χoʤatχona]
ATM	**худпардоз** [χudpardoz]
pharmacy (drugstore)	**дорухона** [doruχona]
hospital	**беморхона** [bemorχona]
police station	**идораи пулис** [idorai pulis]
subway	**метро** [metro]

taxi	**такси** [taksi]
train station	**вокзал** [vokzal]

My name is …	**Номи ман …** [nomi man …]
What's your name?	**Номи шумо чӣ?** [nomi ʃumo tʃi:?]
Could you please help me?	**Илтимос, ба ман ёрӣ диҳед.** [iltimos, ba man jori: dihed]
I've got a problem.	**Ман мушкилӣ дорам.** [man muʃkili: doram]
I don't feel well.	**Худамро бад ҳис мекунам.** [χudamro bad his mekunam]
Call an ambulance!	**Ба ёрии таъҷилӣ занг занед!** [ba jorii ta'dʒili: zang zaned!]
May I make a call?	**Мумкин занг занам?** [mumkin zang zanam?]

I'm sorry.	**Бубахшед** [bubaχʃed]
You're welcome.	**Намеарзад** [namearzad]

I, me	**ман** [man]
you (inform.)	**ту** [tu]
he	**ӯ, вай** [œ, vaj]
she	**ӯ, вай** [œ, vaj]
they (masc.)	**онҳо** [onho]
they (fem.)	**онҳо** [onho]
we	**мо** [mo]
you (pl)	**шумо** [ʃumo]
you (sg, form.)	**Шумо** [ʃumo]

ENTRANCE	**ДАРОМАДГОҲ** [daromadgoh]
EXIT	**БАРОМАДГОҲ** [baromadgoh]
OUT OF ORDER	**КОР НАМЕКУНАД** [kor namekunad]
CLOSED	**ПӮШИДА** [pœʃida]

OPEN	**КУШОДА** [kuʃoda]
FOR WOMEN	**БАРОИ ЗАНОН** [baroi zanon]
FOR MEN	**БАРОИ МАРДОН** [baroi mardon]

TOPICAL
VOCABULARY

This section contains more than 3,000 of the most important words.
The dictionary will provide invaluable assistance while traveling abroad, because frequently individual words are enough for you to be understood.
The dictionary includes a convenient transcription of each foreign word

T&P Books Publishing

VOCABULARY
CONTENTS

T&P Books Publishing

BASIC CONCEPTS

T&P Books Publishing

1. Pronouns

I, me	ман	[man]
you	ту	[tu]
he	ӯ, вай	[œ], [vaj]
she	ӯ, вай	[œ], [vaj]
it	он	[on]
we	мо	[mo]
you (to a group)	шумо	[ʃumo]
you (polite, sing.)	Шумо	[ʃumo]
you (polite, pl)	Шумо	[ʃumo]
they (inanim.)	онон	[onon]
they (anim.)	онҳо, вайҳо	[onho], [vajho]

2. Greetings. Salutations

Hello! (fam.)	Салом!	[salom]
Hello! (form.)	Ассалом!	[assalom]
Good morning!	Субҳатон ба хайр!	[subhaton ba χajr]
Good afternoon!	Рӯз ба хайр!	[rœz ba χajr]
Good evening!	Шом ба хайр!	[ʃom ba χajr]
to say hello	саломалейк кардан	[salomalejk kardan]
Hi! (hello)	Ассалом! Салом!	[assalom salom]
greeting (n)	вохӯрдӣ	[voχœrdi:]
to greet (vt)	вохӯрдӣ кардан	[voχœrdi: kardan]
How are you? (form.)	Корхоятон чӣ хел?	[korhojaton tʃi: χel]
How are you? (fam.)	Корхоят чӣ хел?	[korhojat tʃi: χel]
What's new?	Чӣ навигарӣ?	[tʃi: navigari:]
Goodbye! (form.)	То дидан!	[to didan]
Bye! (fam.)	Хайр!	[χajr]
See you soon!	То вохӯрии наздик!	[to voχœri:i nazdik]
Farewell! (to a friend)	Падруд!	[padrud]
Farewell! (form.)	Хайрбод! Падруд!	[χajrbod padrud]
to say goodbye	падруд гуфтан	[padrud guftan]
So long!	Хайр!	[χajr]
Thank you!	Раҳмат!	[rahmat]
Thank you very much!	Бисёр раҳмат!	[bisjor rahmat]
You're welcome	Марҳамат!	[marhamat]

Don't mention it!	Намеарзад	[namearzad]
It was nothing	Намеарзад	[namearzad]
Excuse me! (fam.)	Бубахш!	[bubaxʃ]
Excuse me! (form.)	Бубахшед!	[bubaxʃed]
to excuse (forgive)	афв кардан	[afv kardan]
to apologize (vi)	узр пурсидан	[uzr pursidan]
My apologies	Маро бубахшед	[maro bubaxʃed]
I'm sorry!	Бубахшед!	[bubaxʃed]
to forgive (vt)	бахшидан	[baxʃidan]
It's okay! (that's all right)	Ҳеч гап не	[hetʃ gap ne]
please (adv)	илтимос	[iltimos]
Don't forget!	Фаромӯш накунед!	[faromœʃ nakuned]
Certainly!	Албатта!	[albatta]
Of course not!	Албатта не!	[albatta ne]
Okay! (I agree)	Розӣ!	[rozi:]
That's enough!	Бас!	[bas]

3. Questions

Who?	Кӣ?	[ki:]
What?	Чӣ?	[tʃi:]
Where? (at, in)	Дар куҷо?	[dar kudʒo]
Where (to)?	Куҷо?	[kudʒo]
From where?	Аз куҷо?	[az kudʒo]
When?	Кай?	[kaj]
Why? (What for?)	Барои чӣ?	[baroi tʃi:]
Why? (~ are you crying?)	Барои чӣ?	[baroi tʃi:]
What for?	Барои чӣ?	[baroi tʃi:]
How? (in what way)	Чӣ хел?	[tʃi: xel]
What? (What kind of ...?)	Кадом?	[kadom]
Which?	Чанд? Чандум?	[tʃand tʃandum]
To whom?	Ба кӣ?	[ba ki:]
About whom?	Дар бораи кӣ?	[dar borai ki:]
About what?	Дар бораи чӣ?	[dar borai tʃi:]
With whom?	Бо кӣ?	[bo ki:]
How many?	Чанд-то?	[tʃand-to]
How much?	Чӣ қадар?	[tʃi: qadar]
Whose?	Аз они кӣ?	[az oni ki:]

4. Prepositions

with (accompanied by)	бо, ҳамроҳи	[bo], [hamrohi]
without	бе	[be]

to (indicating direction)	ба	[ba]
about (talking ~ ...)	дар бораи	[dar borai]
before (in time)	пеш аз	[peʃ az]
in front of ...	дар пеши	[dar peʃi]

under (beneath, below)	таги	[tagi]
above (over)	дар болои	[dar boloi]
on (atop)	ба болои	[ba boloi]
from (off, out of)	аз	[az]
of (made from)	аз	[az]

| in (e.g., ~ ten minutes) | баъд аз | [ba'd az] |
| over (across the top of) | аз болои ... | [az boloi] |

5. Function words. Adverbs. Part 1

Where? (at, in)	Дар куҷо?	[dar kudʒo]
here (adv)	ин ҷо	[in dʒo]
there (adv)	он ҷо	[on dʒo]

| somewhere (to be) | дар куҷое | [dar kudʒoe] |
| nowhere (not anywhere) | дар ҳеҷ ҷо | [dar hedʒ dʒo] |

| by (near, beside) | дар назди ... | [dar nazdi] |
| by the window | дар назди тиреза | [dar nazdi tireza] |

Where (to)?	Куҷо?	[kudʒo]
here (e.g., come ~!)	ин ҷо	[in tʃo]
there (e.g., to go ~)	ба он ҷо	[ba on dʒo]
from here (adv)	аз ин ҷо	[az in dʒo]
from there (adv)	аз он ҷо	[az on dʒo]

| close (adv) | наздик | [nazdik] |
| far (adv) | дур | [dur] |

near (e.g., ~ Paris)	дар бари	[dar bari]
nearby (adv)	бисёр наздик	[bisjor nazdik]
not far (adv)	наздик	[nazdik]

left (adj)	чап	[tʃap]
on the left	аз чап	[az tʃap]
to the left	ба тарафи чап	[ba tarafi tʃap]

right (adj)	рост	[rost]
on the right	аз рост	[az rost]
to the right	ба тарафи рост	[ba tarafi rost]

in front (adv)	аз пеш	[az peʃ]
front (as adj)	пешин	[peʃin]
ahead (the kids ran ~)	ба пеш	[ba peʃ]

behind (adv)	дар қафои	[dar qafoi]
from behind	аз қафо	[az qafo]
back (towards the rear)	ақиб	[aqib]

| middle | миёна | [mijɔna] |
| in the middle | дар миёна | [dar mijɔna] |

at the side	аз паҳлу	[az pahlu]
everywhere (adv)	дар ҳар ҷо	[dar har dʒo]
around (in all directions)	гирду атроф	[girdu atrof]

from inside	аз дарун	[az darun]
somewhere (to go)	ба ким-куҷо	[ba kim-kudʒo]
straight (directly)	миёнбур карда	[mijɔnbur karda]
back (e.g., come ~)	ба ақиб	[ba aqib]

| from anywhere | аз ягон ҷо | [az jagon dʒo] |
| from somewhere | аз як ҷо | [az jak dʒo] |

firstly (adv)	аввалан	[avvalan]
secondly (adv)	дуюм	[dujum]
thirdly (adv)	сеюм	[sejum]

suddenly (adv)	ногоҳ, баногоҳ	[nogoh], [banogoh]
at first (in the beginning)	дар аввал	[dar avval]
for the first time	якумин	[jakumin]
long before ...	хеле пеш	[χele peʃ]
anew (over again)	аз нав	[az nav]
for good (adv)	тамоман	[tamoman]

never (adv)	ҳеҷ гоҳ	[hedʒ goh]
again (adv)	боз, аз дигар	[boz], [az digar]
now (adv)	акнун	[aknun]
often (adv)	тез-тез	[tez-tez]
then (adv)	он вақт	[on vaqt]
urgently (quickly)	зуд, фавран	[zud], [favran]
usually (adv)	одатан	[odatan]

by the way, ...	воқеан	[voqean]
possible (that is ~)	шояд	[ʃojad]
probably (adv)	эҳтимол	[ɛhtimol]
maybe (adv)	эҳтимол, шояд	[ɛhtimol], [ʃojad]
besides ...	ғайр аз он	[ʁajr az on]
that's why ...	бинобар ин	[binobar in]
in spite of ...	ба ин нигоҳ накарда	[ba in nigoh nakarda]
thanks to ...	ба туфайли ...	[ba tufajli]

what (pron.)	чӣ	[tʃiː]
that (conj.)	ки	[ki]
something	чизе	[tʃize]
anything (something)	ягон чиз	[jagon tʃiz]
nothing	ҳеҷ чиз	[hedʒ tʃiz]

who (pron.)	кӣ	[ki:]
someone	ким-кӣ	[kim-ki:]
somebody	касе	[kase]

nobody	ҳеҷ кас	[heʤ kas]
nowhere (a voyage to ~)	ба ҳеҷ куҷо	[ba heʤ kuʤo]
nobody's	бесоҳиб	[besohib]
somebody's	аз они касе	[az oni kase]

so (I'm ~ glad)	чунон	[ʧunon]
also (as well)	ҳам	[ham]
too (as well)	низ, ҳам	[niz], [ham]

6. Function words. Adverbs. Part 2

Why?	Барои чӣ?	[baroi ʧi:]
for some reason	бо ким-кадом сабаб	[bo kim-kadom sabab]
because …	зеро ки	[zero ki]
for some purpose	барои чизе	[baroi ʧize]

and	ва, … у, … ю	[va], [u], [ju]
or	ё	[jɔ]
but	аммо, лекин	[ammo], [lekin]
for (e.g., ~ me)	барои	[baroi]

too (~ many people)	аз меъёр зиёд	[az me'jɔr zijɔd]
only (exclusively)	фақат	[faqat]
exactly (adv)	айнан	[ajnan]
about (more or less)	тақрибан	[taqriban]

approximately (adv)	тақрибан	[taqriban]
approximate (adj)	тақрибӣ	[taqribi:]
almost (adv)	қариб	[qarib]
the rest	боқимонда	[boqimonda]

the other (second)	дигар	[digar]
other (different)	дигар	[digar]
each (adj)	ҳар	[har]
any (no matter which)	ҳар	[har]
many, much (a lot of)	бисёр, хеле	[bisjɔr], [xele]
many people	бисёриҳо	[bisjɔriho]
all (everyone)	ҳама	[hama]

in return for …	ба ивази	[ba ivazi]
in exchange (adv)	ба ивазаш	[ba ivazaʃ]
by hand (made)	дастӣ	[dasti:]
hardly (negative opinion)	ба гумон	[ba gumon]

| probably (adv) | эҳтимол, шояд | [ɛhtimol], [ʃojad] |
| on purpose (intentionally) | барқасд | [barqasd] |

by accident (adv)	тасодуфан	[tasodufan]
very (adv)	хеле	[χele]
for example (adv)	масалан, чунончи	[masalan], [tʃunontʃi]
between	дар байни	[dar bajni]
among	дар байни …	[dar bajni]
so much (such a lot)	ин қадар	[in qadar]
especially (adv)	хусусан	[χususan]

NUMBERS. MISCELLANEOUS

T&P Books Publishing

7. Cardinal numbers. Part 1

0 zero	сифр	[sifr]
1 one	як	[jak]
2 two	ду	[du]
3 three	се	[se]
4 four	чор, чаҳор	[tʃor], [tʃahor]
5 five	панҷ	[pandʒ]
6 six	шаш	[ʃaʃ]
7 seven	ҳафт	[haft]
8 eight	ҳашт	[haʃt]
9 nine	нуҳ	[nuh]
10 ten	даҳ	[dah]
11 eleven	ёздаҳ	[jozdah]
12 twelve	дувоздаҳ	[duvozdah]
13 thirteen	сездаҳ	[sezdah]
14 fourteen	чордаҳ	[tʃordah]
15 fifteen	понздаҳ	[ponzdah]
16 sixteen	шонздаҳ	[ʃonzdah]
17 seventeen	ҳафдаҳ	[hafdah]
18 eighteen	ҳаждаҳ	[haʒdah]
19 nineteen	нуздаҳ	[nuzdah]
20 twenty	бист	[bist]
21 twenty-one	бисту як	[bistu jak]
22 twenty-two	бисту ду	[bistu du]
23 twenty-three	бисту се	[bistu se]
30 thirty	сӣ	[siː]
31 thirty-one	сию як	[siju jak]
32 thirty-two	сию ду	[siju du]
33 thirty-three	сию се	[siju se]
40 forty	чил	[tʃil]
41 forty-one	чилу як	[tʃilu jak]
42 forty-two	чилу ду	[tʃilu du]
43 forty-three	чилу се	[tʃilu se]
50 fifty	панҷоҳ	[pandʒoh]
51 fifty-one	панҷоҳу як	[pandʒohu jak]
52 fifty-two	панҷоҳу ду	[pandʒohu du]
53 fifty-three	панҷоҳу се	[pandʒohu se]
60 sixty	шаст	[ʃast]

61 sixty-one	шасту як	[ʃastu jak]
62 sixty-two	шасту ду	[ʃastu du]
63 sixty-three	шасту се	[ʃastu se]

70 seventy	ҳафтод	[haftod]
71 seventy-one	ҳафтоду як	[haftodu jak]
72 seventy-two	ҳафтоду ду	[haftodu du]
73 seventy-three	ҳафтоду се	[haftodu se]

80 eighty	ҳаштод	[haʃtod]
81 eighty-one	ҳаштоду як	[haʃtodu jak]
82 eighty-two	ҳаштоду ду	[haʃtodu du]
83 eighty-three	ҳаштоду се	[haʃtodu se]

90 ninety	навад	[navad]
91 ninety-one	наваду як	[navadu jak]
92 ninety-two	наваду ду	[navadu du]
93 ninety-three	наваду се	[navadu se]

8. Cardinal numbers. Part 2

100 one hundred	сад	[sad]
200 two hundred	дусад	[dusad]
300 three hundred	сесад	[sesad]
400 four hundred	чорсад, чаҳорсад	[tʃorsad], [tʃahorsad]
500 five hundred	панҷсад	[pandʒsad]

600 six hundred	шашсад	[ʃaʃsad]
700 seven hundred	ҳафтсад	[haftsad]
800 eight hundred	ҳаштсад	[haʃtsad]
900 nine hundred	нӯҳсадум	[nœhsadum]

1000 one thousand	ҳазор	[hazor]
2000 two thousand	ду ҳазор	[du hazor]
3000 three thousand	се ҳазор	[se hazor]
10000 ten thousand	даҳ ҳазор	[dah hazor]
one hundred thousand	сад ҳазор	[sad hazor]
million	миллион	[million]
billion	миллиард	[milliard]

9. Ordinal numbers

first (adj)	якум	[jakum]
second (adj)	дуюм	[dujum]
third (adj)	сеюм	[sejum]
fourth (adj)	чорум	[tʃorum]
fifth (adj)	панчум	[pandʒum]
sixth (adj)	шашум	[ʃaʃum]

seventh (adj)	**ҳафтум**	[haftum]
eighth (adj)	**ҳаштум**	[haʃtum]
ninth (adj)	**нӯҳум**	[nœhum]
tenth (adj)	**даҳӯм**	[dahœm]

COLOURS. UNITS OF MEASUREMENT

T&P Books Publishing

10. Colors

color	ранг	[rang]
shade (tint)	тобиш	[tobiʃ]
hue	тобиш, лавн	[tobiʃ], [lavn]
rainbow	рангинкамон	[ranginkamon]

white (adj)	сафед	[safed]
black (adj)	сиёх	[sijɔh]
gray (adj)	адкан	[adkan]

green (adj)	сабз, кабуд	[sabz], [kabud]
yellow (adj)	зард	[zard]
red (adj)	сурх, аргувонй	[surχ], [arʁuvoni:]
blue (adj)	кабуд	[kabud]
light blue (adj)	осмонй	[osmoni:]
pink (adj)	гулобй	[gulobi:]
orange (adj)	норанчй	[norandʒi:]
violet (adj)	бунафш	[bunafʃ]
brown (adj)	қаҳвагй	[qahvagi:]

golden (adj)	тиллоранг	[tillorang]
silvery (adj)	нуқрафом	[nuqrafom]
beige (adj)	каҳваранг	[kahvarang]
cream (adj)	зардтоб	[zardtob]
turquoise (adj)	фирӯзаранг	[firœzarang]
cherry red (adj)	олуболугй	[olubolugi:]
lilac (adj)	бунафш, нофармон	[bunafʃ], [nofarmon]
crimson (adj)	сурхи сиеҳтоб	[surχi siehtob]

light (adj)	кушод	[kuʃod]
dark (adj)	торик	[torik]
bright, vivid (adj)	тоза	[toza]

colored (pencils)	ранга	[ranga]
color (e.g., ~ film)	ранга	[ranga]
black-and-white (adj)	сиёху сафед	[sijɔhu safed]
plain (one-colored)	якранга	[jakranga]
multicolored (adj)	рангоранг	[rangorang]

11. Units of measurement

weight	вазн	[vazn]
length	дарозй	[darozi:]

width	арз	[arz]
height	баландӣ	[balandi:]
depth	чуқурӣ	[tʃuquri:]
volume	ҳаҷм	[hadʒm]
area	масоҳат	[masohat]

gram	грам	[gram]
milligram	миллиграмм	[milligramm]
kilogram	килограмм	[kilogramm]
ton	тонна	[tonna]
pound	қадоқ	[qadoq]
ounce	вақия	[vaqija]

meter	метр	[metr]
millimeter	миллиметр	[millimetr]
centimeter	сантиметр	[santimetr]
kilometer	километр	[kilometr]
mile	мил	[mil]

foot	фут	[fut]
yard	ярд	[jard]

square meter	метри квадратӣ	[metri kvadrati:]
hectare	гектар	[gektar]

liter	литр	[litr]
degree	дараҷа	[daradʒa]
volt	волт	[volt]
ampere	ампер	[amper]
horsepower	қувваи асп	[quvvai asp]

quantity	миқдор	[miqdor]
a little bit of …	камтар	[kamtar]
half	нисф	[nisf]
piece (item)	дона	[dona]

size	ҳаҷм	[hadʒm]
scale (map ~)	масштаб	[masʃtab]

minimal (adj)	камтарин	[kamtarin]
the smallest (adj)	хурдтарин	[χurdtarin]
medium (adj)	миёна	[mijɔna]
maximal (adj)	ниҳоят калон	[nihojat kalon]
the largest (adj)	калонтарин	[kalontarin]

12. Containers

canning jar (glass ~)	банкаи шишагӣ	[bankai ʃiʃagi:]
can	банкаи тунукагӣ	[bankai tunukagi:]
bucket	сатил	[satil]

barrel	бочка, чалак	[botʃka], [tʃalak]
wash basin (e.g., plastic ~)	тағора	[taʁora]
tank (100L water ~)	бак, чалак	[bak], [tʃalak]
hip flask	обдон	[obdon]
jerrycan	канистра	[kanistra]
tank (e.g., tank car)	систерна	[sisterna]

mug	кружка, дӯлча	[kruʒka], [dœltʃa]
cup (of coffee, etc.)	косача	[kosatʃa]
saucer	тақсимӣ, тақсимича	[taqsimi:], [taqsimitʃa]
glass (tumbler)	стакан	[stakan]
wine glass	бокал	[bokal]
stock pot (soup pot)	дегча	[degtʃa]

| bottle (~ of wine) | шиша, сурохӣ | [ʃiʃa], [surohi:] |
| neck (of the bottle, etc.) | даҳани шиша | [dahani ʃiʃa] |

carafe (decanter)	сурохӣ	[surohi:]
pitcher	кӯза	[kœza]
vessel (container)	зарф	[zarf]
pot (crock, stoneware ~)	хурмача	[χurmatʃa]
vase	гулдон	[guldon]

bottle (perfume ~)	шиша	[ʃiʃa]
vial, small bottle	ҳубобча	[hubobtʃa]
tube (of toothpaste)	лӯлача	[lœlatʃa]

sack (bag)	халта	[χalta]
bag (paper ~, plastic ~)	халта	[χalta]
pack (of cigarettes, etc.)	қуттӣ	[qutti:]

box (e.g., shoebox)	қуттӣ	[qutti:]
crate	қуттӣ	[qutti:]
basket	сабад	[sabad]

MAIN VERBS

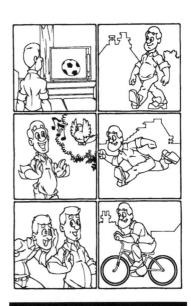

T&P Books Publishing

13. The most important verbs. Part 1

to advise (vt)	маслиҳат додан	[maslihat dodan]
to agree (say yes)	розигӣ додан	[rozigi: dodan]
to answer (vi, vt)	ҷавоб додан	[dʒavob dodan]
to apologize (vi)	узр пурсидан	[uzr pursidan]
to arrive (vi)	расидан	[rasidan]
to ask (~ oneself)	пурсидан	[pursidan]
to ask (~ sb to do sth)	пурсидан	[pursidan]
to be (vi)	будан	[budan]
to be afraid	тарсидан	[tarsidan]
to be hungry	хӯрок хостан	[χœrok χostan]
to be interested in …	ҳавас кардан	[havas kardan]
to be needed	даркор будан	[darkor budan]
to be surprised	ба ҳайрат афтодан	[ba hajrat aftodan]
to be thirsty	об хостан	[ob χostan]
to begin (vt)	сар кардан	[sar kardan]
to belong to …	таалуқ доштан	[taaluq doʃtan]
to boast (vi)	худситой кардан	[χudsitoi: kardan]
to break (split into pieces)	шикастан	[ʃikastan]
to call (~ for help)	чеғ задан	[dʒeʁ zadan]
can (v aux)	тавонистан	[tavonistan]
to catch (vt)	доштан	[doʃtan]
to change (vt)	иваз кардан	[ivaz kardan]
to choose (select)	интихоб кардан	[intiχob kardan]
to come down (the stairs)	фуромадан	[furomadan]
to compare (vt)	муқоиса кардан	[muqoisa kardan]
to complain (vi, vt)	шикоят кардан	[ʃikojat kardan]
to confuse (mix up)	иштибоҳ кардан	[iʃtiboh kardan]
to continue (vt)	давомат кардан	[davomat kardan]
to control (vt)	назорат кардан	[nazorat kardan]
to cook (dinner)	пухтан	[puχtan]
to cost (vt)	арзидан	[arzidan]
to count (add up)	ҳисоб кардан	[hisob kardan]
to count on …	умед бастан	[umed bastan]
to create (vt)	офаридан	[ofaridan]
to cry (weep)	гиря кардан	[girja kardan]

14. The most important verbs. Part 2

to deceive (vi, vt)	фирефтан	[fireftan]
to decorate (tree, street)	оростан	[orostan]
to defend (a country, etc.)	муҳофиза кардан	[muhofiza kardan]
to demand (request firmly)	талаб кардан	[talab kardan]
to dig (vt)	кофтан	[koftan]
to discuss (vt)	муҳокима кардан	[muhokima kardan]
to do (vt)	кардан	[kardan]
to doubt (have doubts)	шак доштан	[ʃak doʃtan]
to drop (let fall)	афтондан	[aftondan]
to enter (room, house, etc.)	даромадан	[daromadan]
to excuse (forgive)	афв кардан	[afv kardan]
to exist (vi)	зиндагӣ кардан	[zindagi: kardan]
to expect (foresee)	пешбинӣ кардан	[peʃbini: kardan]
to explain (vt)	шарҳ додан	[ʃarh dodan]
to fall (vi)	афтодан	[aftodan]
to find (vt)	ёфтан	[joftan]
to finish (vt)	тамом кардан	[tamom kardan]
to fly (vi)	паридан	[paridan]
to follow ... (come after)	рафтан	[raftan]
to forget (vi, vt)	фаромӯш кардан	[faromœʃ kardan]
to forgive (vt)	бахшидан	[baχʃidan]
to give (vt)	додан	[dodan]
to give a hint	луқма додан	[luqma dodan]
to go (on foot)	рафтан	[raftan]
to go for a swim	оббозӣ кардан	[obbozi: kardan]
to go out (for dinner, etc.)	баромадан	[baromadan]
to guess (the answer)	ёфтан	[joftan]
to have (vt)	доштан	[doʃtan]
to have breakfast	ноништа кардан	[noniʃta kardan]
to have dinner	хӯроки шом хӯрдан	[χœroki ʃom χœrdan]
to have lunch	хӯроки пешин хӯрдан	[χœroki peʃin χœrdan]
to hear (vt)	шунидан	[ʃunidan]
to help (vt)	кумак кардан	[kumak kardan]
to hide (vt)	пинҳон кардан	[pinhon kardan]
to hope (vi, vt)	умед доштан	[umed doʃtan]
to hunt (vi, vt)	шикор кардан	[ʃikor kardan]
to hurry (vi)	шитоб кардан	[ʃitob kardan]

15. The most important verbs. Part 3

to inform (vt)	ахборот додан	[aχborot dodan]
to insist (vi, vt)	сахт истодан	[saχt istodan]
to insult (vt)	таҳқир кардан	[tahqir kardan]
to invite (vt)	даъват кардан	[da'vat kardan]
to joke (vi)	шӯхӣ кардан	[ʃœχi: kardan]

to keep (vt)	нигоҳ доштан	[nigoh doʃtan]
to keep silent	хомӯш будан	[χomœʃ budan]
to kill (vt)	куштан	[kuʃtan]
to know (sb)	донистан	[donistan]
to know (sth)	донистан	[donistan]
to laugh (vi)	хандидан	[χandidan]

to liberate (city, etc.)	озод кардан	[ozod kardan]
to like (I like …)	форидан	[foridan]
to look for … (search)	ҷустан	[dʒustan]
to love (sb)	дӯст доштан	[dœst doʃtan]
to make a mistake	хато кардан	[χato kardan]
to manage, to run	сардорӣ кардан	[sardori: kardan]
to mean (signify)	маъно доштан	[ma'no doʃtan]
to mention (talk about)	гуфта гузаштан	[gufta guzaʃtan]
to miss (school, etc.)	набудан	[nabudan]
to notice (see)	дида мондан	[dida mondan]

to object (vi, vt)	зид баромадан	[zid baromadan]
to observe (see)	назорат кардан	[nazorat kardan]
to open (vt)	кушодан	[kuʃodan]
to order (meal, etc.)	супоридан	[suporidan]
to order (mil.)	фармон додан	[farmon dodan]
to own (possess)	соҳиб будан	[sohib budan]
to participate (vi)	иштирок кардан	[iʃtirok kardan]
to pay (vi, vt)	пул додан	[pul dodan]
to permit (vt)	иҷозат додан	[idʒozat dodan]
to plan (vt)	нақша кашидан	[naqʃa kaʃidan]
to play (children)	бозӣ кардан	[bozi: kardan]

to pray (vi, vt)	намоз хондан	[namoz χondan]
to prefer (vt)	беҳтар донистан	[beχtar donistan]
to promise (vt)	ваъда додан	[va'da dodan]
to pronounce (vt)	талаффуз кардан	[talaffuz kardan]
to propose (vt)	таклиф кардан	[taklif kardan]
to punish (vt)	ҷазо додан	[dʒazo dodan]

16. The most important verbs. Part 4

| to read (vi, vt) | хондан | [χondan] |
| to recommend (vt) | маслиҳат додан | [maslihat dodan] |

to refuse (vi, vt)	рад кардан	[rad kardan]
to regret (be sorry)	таассуф хӯрдан	[taassuf χœrdan]
to rent (sth from sb)	ба иҷора гирифтан	[ba idʒora giriftan]
to repeat (say again)	такрор кардан	[takror kardan]
to reserve, to book	нигоҳ доштан	[nigoh doʃtan]
to run (vi)	давидан	[davidan]
to save (rescue)	наҷот додан	[nadʒot dodan]
to say (~ thank you)	гуфтан	[guftan]
to scold (vt)	дашном додан	[daʃnom dodan]
to see (vt)	дидан	[didan]
to sell (vt)	фурӯхтан	[furœχtan]
to send (vt)	ирсол кардан	[irsol kardan]
to shoot (vi)	тир задан	[tir zadan]
to shout (vi)	дод задан	[dod zadan]
to show (vt)	нишон додан	[niʃon dodan]
to sign (document)	имзо кардан	[imzo kardan]
to sit down (vi)	нишастан	[niʃastan]
to smile (vi)	табассум кардан	[tabassum kardan]
to speak (vi, vt)	гап задан	[gap zadan]
to steal (money, etc.)	дуздидан	[duzdidan]
to stop (for pause, etc.)	истодан	[istodan]
to stop (please ~ calling me)	бас кардан	[bas kardan]
to study (vt)	омӯхтан	[omœχtan]
to swim (vi)	шино кардан	[ʃino kardan]
to take (vt)	гирифтан	[giriftan]
to think (vi, vt)	фикр кардан	[fikr kardan]
to threaten (vt)	дӯғ задан	[dœʁ zadan]
to touch (with hands)	даст расондан	[dast rasondan]
to translate (vt)	тарҷума кардан	[tardʒuma kardan]
to trust (vt)	бовар кардан	[bovar kardan]
to try (attempt)	озмоиш кардан	[ozmoiʃ kardan]
to turn (e.g., ~ left)	гардонидан	[gardonidan]
to underestimate (vt)	хунукназарӣ кардан	[χunuknazari: kardan]
to understand (vt)	фаҳмидан	[fahmidan]
to unite (vt)	якҷоя кардан	[jakdʒoja kardan]
to wait (vt)	поидан	[poidan]
to want (wish, desire)	хостан	[χostan]
to warn (vt)	танбеҳ додан	[tanbeh dodan]
to work (vi)	кор кардан	[kor kardan]
to write (vt)	навиштан	[naviʃtan]
to write down	навиштан	[naviʃtan]

TIME. CALENDAR

T&P Books Publishing

17. Weekdays

Monday	душанбе	[duʃanbe]
Tuesday	сешанбе	[seʃanbe]
Wednesday	чоршанбе	[tʃorʃanbe]
Thursday	панчшанбе	[pandʒʃanbe]
Friday	чумъа	[dʒum'a]
Saturday	шанбе	[ʃanbe]
Sunday	якшанбе	[jakʃanbe]

today (adv)	имрӯз	[imrœz]
tomorrow (adv)	пагох, фардо	[pagoh], [fardo]
the day after tomorrow	пасфардо	[pasfardo]
yesterday (adv)	дирӯз, дина	[dirœz], [dina]
the day before yesterday	парирӯз	[parirœz]

day	рӯз	[rœz]
working day	рӯзи кор	[rœzi kor]
public holiday	рӯзи ид	[rœzi id]
day off	рӯзи истирохат	[rœzi istirohat]
weekend	рӯзхои истирохат	[rœzhoi istirohat]

all day long	тамоми рӯз	[tamomi rœz]
the next day (adv)	рӯзи дигар	[rœzi digar]
two days ago	ду рӯз пеш	[du rœz peʃ]
the day before	як рӯз пеш	[jak rœz peʃ]
daily (adj)	харрӯза	[harrœza]
every day (adv)	хар рӯз	[har rœz]

week	хафта	[hafta]
last week (adv)	хафтаи гузашта	[haftai guzaʃta]
next week (adv)	хафтаи оянда	[haftai ojanda]
weekly (adj)	хафтаина	[haftaina]
every week (adv)	хар хафта	[har hafta]
twice a week	хафтае ду маротиба	[haftae du marotiba]
every Tuesday	хар сешанбе	[har seʃanbe]

18. Hours. Day and night

morning	пагохӣ	[pagohi:]
in the morning	пагохирӯзӣ	[pagohirœzi:]
noon, midday	нисфи рӯз	[nisfi rœz]
in the afternoon	баъди пешин	[ba'di peʃin]
evening	бегох, бегохирӯз	[begoh], [begohirœz]

in the evening	бегоҳӣ, бегоҳирӯзӣ	[begohi:], [begohirœzi:]
night	шаб	[ʃab]
at night	шабона	[ʃabona]
midnight	нисфи шаб	[nisfi ʃab]

second	сония	[sonija]
minute	дақиқа	[daqiqa]
hour	соат	[soat]
half an hour	нимсоат	[nimsoat]
a quarter-hour	чоряки соат	[tʃorjaki soat]
fifteen minutes	понздаҳ дақиқа	[ponzdah daqiqa]
24 hours	шабонарӯз	[ʃabonarœz]

sunrise	тулӯъ	[tulœ']
dawn	субҳидам	[subhidam]
early morning	субҳи барвақт	[subhi barvaqt]
sunset	ғуруби офтоб	[ʁurubi oftob]

early in the morning	субҳи барвақт	[subhi barvaqt]
this morning	имрӯз пагоҳӣ	[imrœz pagohi:]
tomorrow morning	пагоҳ саҳарӣ	[pagoh sahari:]

this afternoon	имрӯз	[imrœz]
in the afternoon	баъди пешин	[ba'di peʃin]
tomorrow afternoon	пагоҳ баъди пешин	[pagoh ba'di peʃin]

| tonight (this evening) | ҳамин бегоҳ | [hamin begoh] |
| tomorrow night | фардо бегоҳӣ | [fardo begohi:] |

at 3 o'clock sharp	расо соати се	[raso soati se]
about 4 o'clock	наздикии соати чор	[nazdiki:i soati tʃor]
by 12 o'clock	соатҳои дувоздаҳ	[soathoi duvozdah]

in 20 minutes	баъд аз бист дақиқа	[ba'd az bist daqiqa]
in an hour	баъд аз як соат	[ba'd az jak soat]
on time (adv)	дар вақташ	[dar vaqtaʃ]

a quarter of ...	понздаҳто кам	[ponzdahto kam]
within an hour	дар давоми як соат	[dar davomi jak soat]
every 15 minutes	ҳар понздаҳ дақиқа	[har ponzdah daqiqa]
round the clock	шабу рӯз	[ʃabu rœz]

19. Months. Seasons

January	январ	[janvar]
February	феврал	[fevral]
March	март	[mart]
April	апрел	[aprel]
May	май	[maj]
June	июн	[ijun]

July	июл	[ijul]
August	август	[avgust]
September	сентябр	[sentjabr]
October	октябр	[oktjabr]
November	ноябр	[nojabr]
December	декабр	[dekabr]

spring	баҳор, баҳорон	[bahor], [bahoron]
in spring	дар фасли баҳор	[dar fasli bahor]
spring (as adj)	баҳорӣ	[bahori:]

summer	тобистон	[tobiston]
in summer	дар тобистон	[dar tobiston]
summer (as adj)	тобистона	[tobistona]

fall	тирамоҳ	[tiramoh]
in fall	дар тирамоҳ	[dar tiramoh]
fall (as adj)	… и тирамоҳ	[i tiramoh]

winter	зимистон	[zimiston]
in winter	дар зимистон	[dar zimiston]
winter (as adj)	зимистонӣ, … и зимистон	[zimistoni:], [i zimiston]

month	моҳ	[moh]
this month	ҳамин моҳ	[hamin moh]
next month	дар моҳи оянда	[dar mohi ojanda]
last month	дар моҳи гузашта	[dar mohi guzaʃta]

a month ago	як моҳ пеш	[jak moh peʃ]
in a month (a month later)	баъд аз як моҳ	[ba'd az jak moh]
in 2 months (2 months later)	баъд аз ду моҳ	[ba'd az du moh]
the whole month	тамоми моҳ	[tamomi moh]
all month long	тамоми моҳ	[tamomi moh]

monthly (~ magazine)	ҳармоҳа	[harmoha]
monthly (adv)	ҳар моҳ	[har moh]
every month	ҳар моҳ	[har moh]
twice a month	ду маротиба дар як моҳ	[du marotiba dar jak moh]

year	сол	[sol]
this year	ҳамин сол	[hamin sol]
next year	соли оянда	[soli ojanda]
last year	соли гузашта	[soli guzaʃta]

a year ago	як сол пеш	[jak sol peʃ]
in a year	баъд аз як сол	[ba'd az jak sol]
in two years	баъд аз ду сол	[ba'd az du sol]
the whole year	тамоми сол	[tamomi sol]
all year long	як соли пурра	[jak soli purra]
every year	ҳар сол	[har sol]

annual (adj)	харсола	[harsola]
annually (adv)	ҳар сол	[har sol]
4 times a year	чор маротиба	[tʃor marotiba
	дар як сол	dar jak sol]

date (e.g., today's ~)	таърих, рӯз	[ta'riχ], [rœz]
date (e.g., ~ of birth)	сана	[sana]
calendar	тақвим, солнома	[taqvim], [solnoma]

half a year	ним сол	[nim sol]
six months	нимсола	[nimsola]
season (summer, etc.)	фасл	[fasl]
century	аср	[asr]

TRAVEL. HOTEL

T&P Books Publishing

20. Trip. Travel

tourism, travel	туризм, саёхат	[turizm], [sajɔχat]
tourist	саёҳатчй	[sajɔhatʧi:]
trip, voyage	саёҳат	[sajɔhat]
adventure	саргузашт	[sarguzaʃt]
trip, journey	сафар	[safar]
vacation	рухсатй	[ruχsati:]
to be on vacation	дар рухсатй будан	[dar ruχsati: budan]
rest	истироҳат	[istirohat]
train	поезд, қатор	[poezd], [qator]
by train	бо қатора	[bo qatora]
airplane	ҳавопаймо	[havopajmo]
by airplane	бо ҳавопаймо	[bo havopajmo]
by car	бо мошин	[bo moʃin]
by ship	бо киштй	[bo kiʃti:]
luggage	бағоч, бор	[baʁoʤ], [bor]
suitcase	чомадон	[ʤomadon]
luggage cart	аробаи боғочкашй	[arobai boʁoʧkaʃi:]
passport	шиноснома	[ʃinosnoma]
visa	виза	[viza]
ticket	билет	[bilet]
air ticket	чиптаи ҳавопаймо	[ʧiptai havopajmo]
guidebook	роҳнома	[rohnoma]
map (tourist ~)	харита	[χarita]
area (rural ~)	чой, маҳал	[ʤoj], [mahal]
place, site	чой	[ʤoj]
exotica (n)	ғароибот	[ʁaroibot]
exotic (adj)	... и ғароиб	[i ʁaroib]
amazing (adj)	ҳайратангез	[hajratangez]
group	гурӯҳ	[gurœh]
excursion, sightseeing tour	экскурсия, саёҳат	[ɛkskursija], [sajɔhat]
guide (person)	роҳбари экскурсия	[rohbari ɛkskursija]

21. Hotel

hotel	меҳмонхона	[mehmonχona]
motel	меҳмонхона	[mehmonχona]

three-star (~ hotel)	се ситорадор	[se sitorador]
five-star	панҷ ситорадор	[pandʒ sitorador]
to stay (in a hotel, etc.)	фуромадан	[furomadan]
room	хуҷра	[hudʒra]
single room	хуҷраи якнафара	[hudʒrai jaknafara]
double room	хуҷраи дунафара	[hudʒrai dunafara]
to book a room	банд кардани хуҷра	[band kardani hudʒra]
half board	бо нимтаъминот	[bo nimta'minot]
full board	бо таъминоти пурра	[bo ta'minoti purra]
with bath	ваннадор	[vannador]
with shower	душдор	[duʃdor]
satellite television	телевизиони спутникй	[televizioni sputniki:]
air-conditioner	кондитсионер	[konditsioner]
towel	сачоқ	[satʃoq]
key	калид	[kalid]
administrator	маъмур, мудир	[ma'mur], [mudir]
chambermaid	пешхизмат	[peʃxizmat]
porter, bellboy	ҳаммол	[hammol]
doorman	дарбони меҳмонхона	[darboni mehmonχona]
restaurant	тарабхона	[tarabχona]
pub, bar	бар	[bar]
breakfast	ноништа	[noniʃta]
dinner	шом	[ʃom]
buffet	мизи шведй	[mizi ʃvedi:]
lobby	миёнсарой	[mijɔnsaroj]
elevator	лифт	[lift]
DO NOT DISTURB	ХАЛАЛ НАРАСОНЕД	[χalal narasoned]
NO SMOKING	ТАМОКУ НАКАШЕД!	[tamoku nakaʃed]

22. Sightseeing

monument	ҳайкал	[hajkal]
fortress	ҳисор	[hisor]
palace	қаср	[qasr]
castle	кӯшк	[kœʃk]
tower	манора, бурҷ	[manora], [burdʒ]
mausoleum	мавзолей, мақбара	[mavzolej], [maqbara]
architecture	меъморй	[me'mori:]
medieval (adj)	асримиёнагй	[asrimijɔnagi:]
ancient (adj)	қадим	[qadim]
national (adj)	миллй	[milli:]
famous (monument, etc.)	маъруф	[ma'ruf]

tourist	саёҳатчй	[sajɔhattʃi:]
guide (person)	роҳбалад	[rohbalad]
excursion, sightseeing tour	экскурсия	[ɛkskursija]
to show (vt)	нишон додан	[niʃon dodan]
to tell (vt)	нақл кардан	[naql kardan]

to find (vt)	ёфтан	[jɔftan]
to get lost (lose one's way)	роҳ гум кардан	[roh gum kardan]
map (e.g., subway ~)	накша	[nakʃa]
map (e.g., city ~)	нақша	[naqʃa]

souvenir, gift	тӯҳфа	[tœhfa]
gift shop	мағозаи туҳфаҳо	[maʁozai tuhfaho]
to take pictures	сурат гирифтан	[surat giriftan]
to have one's picture taken	сурати худро гирондан	[surati χudro girondan]

TRANSPORTATION

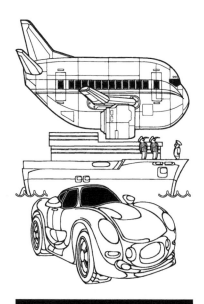

T&P Books Publishing

airport	аэропорт	[aɛroport]
airplane	ҳавопаймо	[havopajmo]
airline	ширкати ҳавопаймой	[ʃirkati havopajmoi:]
air traffic controller	диспечер	[dispetʃer]

departure	парвоз	[parvoz]
arrival	парида омадан	[parida omadan]
to arrive (by plane)	парида омадан	[parida omadan]

departure time	вақти паридан	[vaqti paridan]
arrival time	вақти шиштан	[vaqti ʃiʃtan]

to be delayed	боздоштан	[bozdoʃtan]
flight delay	боздоштани парвоз	[bozdoʃtani parvoz]

information board	тахтаи ахборот	[taχtai aχborot]
information	ахборот	[aχborot]
to announce (vt)	эълон кардан	[ɛ'lon kardan]
flight (e.g., next ~)	сафар, рейс	[safar], [rejs]

customs	гумрукхона	[gumrukχona]
customs officer	гумрукчӣ	[gumruktʃi:]

customs declaration	декларатсияи гумрукӣ	[deklaratsijai gumruki:]
to fill out (vt)	пур кардан	[pur kardan]
to fill out the declaration	пур кардани декларатсия	[pur kardani deklaratsija]
passport control	назорати шиносноma	[nazorati ʃinosnoma]

luggage	бағоҷ, бор	[baʁodʒ], [bor]
hand luggage	бори дастӣ	[bori dasti:]
luggage cart	аробаи бағочкашӣ	[arobai baʁotʃkaʃi:]

landing	фуруд	[furud]
landing strip	хати нишаст	[χati niʃast]
to land (vi)	нишастан	[niʃastan]
airstairs	зинапояи киштӣ	[zinapojai kiʃti:]

check-in	бақайдгирӣ	[baqajdgiri:]
check-in counter	қатори бақайдгирӣ	[qatori baqajdgiri:]
to check-in (vi)	қайд кунондан	[qajd kunondan]
boarding pass	талони саворшавӣ	[taloni savorʃavi:]
departure gate	баромадан	[baromadan]
transit	транзит	[tranzit]

to wait (vt)	поидан	[poidan]
departure lounge	толори интизорӣ	[tolori intizori:]
to see off	гусел кардан	[gusel kardan]
to say goodbye	падруд гуфтан	[padrud guftan]

24. Airplane

airplane	ҳавопаймо	[havopajmo]
air ticket	чиптаи ҳавопаймо	[tʃiptai havopajmo]
airline	ширкати ҳавопаймой	[ʃirkati havopajmoi:]
airport	аэропорт	[aɛroport]
supersonic (adj)	фавқуссадо	[favqussado]

captain	фармондеҳи киштӣ	[farmondehi kiʃti:]
crew	экипаж	[ɛkipaʒ]
pilot	сарнишин	[sarniʃin]
flight attendant (fem.)	стюардесса	[stjuardessa]
navigator	штурман	[ʃturman]

wings	қанот	[qanot]
tail	дум	[dum]
cockpit	кабина	[kabina]
engine	муҳаррик	[muharrik]
undercarriage (landing gear)	шассӣ	[ʃassi:]
turbine	турбина	[turbina]

propeller	пропеллер	[propeller]
black box	қуттии сиёҳ	[qutti:i sijɔh]
yoke (control column)	суккон	[sukkon]
fuel	сӯзишворӣ	[sœziʃvori:]

safety card	дастурамали бехатарӣ	[dasturamali beχatari:]
oxygen mask	ниқоби ҳавои тоза	[niqobi havoi toza]
uniform	либоси расмӣ	[libosi rasmi:]
life vest	камзӯли наҷотдиҳанда	[kamzœli nadʒotdihanda]
parachute	парашют	[paraʃut]

takeoff	парвоз	[parvoz]
to take off (vi)	парвоз кардан	[parvoz kardan]
runway	хати парвоз	[χati parvoz]

visibility	софии ҳаво	[sofi:i havo]
flight (act of flying)	парвоз	[parvoz]
altitude	баландӣ	[balandi:]
air pocket	чоҳи ҳаво	[tʃohi havo]

seat	ҷой	[dʒoj]
headphones	гӯшак, гӯшпӯшак	[gœʃak], [gœʃpœʃak]
folding tray (tray table)	мизчаи вошаванда	[miztʃai voʃavanda]

airplane window	иллюминатор	[illjuminator]
aisle	гузаргоҳ	[guzargoh]

25. Train

train	поезд, қатор	[poezd], [qator]
commuter train	қатораи барқӣ	[qatorai barqi:]
express train	қатораи тезгард	[qatorai tezgard]
diesel locomotive	тепловоз	[teplovoz]
steam locomotive	паровоз	[parovoz]
passenger car	вагон	[vagon]
dining car	вагон-ресторан	[vagon-restoran]
rails	релсҳо	[relsho]
railroad	роҳи оҳан	[rohi ohan]
railway tie	шпала	[ʃpala]
platform (railway ~)	платформа	[platforma]
track (~ 1, 2, etc.)	роҳ	[roh]
semaphore	семафор	[semafor]
station	истгоҳ	[istgoh]
engineer (train driver)	мошинист	[moʃinist]
porter (of luggage)	ҳаммол	[hammol]
car attendant	роҳбалад	[rohbalad]
passenger	мусофир	[musofir]
conductor (ticket inspector)	нозир	[nozir]
corridor (in train)	коридор	[koridor]
emergency brake	стоп-кран	[stop-kran]
compartment	купе	[kupe]
berth	кат	[kat]
upper berth	кати боло	[kati bolo]
lower berth	кати поён	[kati pojɔn]
bed linen, bedding	ҷилдҳои болишту бистар	[dʒildhoi boliʃtu bistar]
ticket	билет	[bilet]
schedule	ҷадвал	[dʒadval]
information display	ҷадвал	[dʒadval]
to leave, to depart	дур шудан	[dur ʃudan]
departure (of train)	равон кардан	[ravon kardan]
to arrive (ab. train)	омадан	[omadan]
arrival	омадан	[omadan]
to arrive by train	бо қатора омадан	[bo qatora omadan]
to get on the train	ба қатора нишастан	[ba qatora niʃastan]

to get off the train	фаромадан	[faromadan]
train wreck	садама	[sadama]
to derail (vi)	аз релс баромадан	[az rels baromadan]

steam locomotive	паровоз	[parovoz]
stoker, fireman	алавмон	[alavmon]
firebox	оташдон	[otaʃdon]
coal	ангишт	[angiʃt]

26. Ship

| ship | киштӣ | [kiʃti:] |
| vessel | киштӣ | [kiʃti:] |

steamship	пароход	[paroχod]
riverboat	теплоход	[teploχod]
cruise ship	лайнер	[lajner]
cruiser	крейсер	[krejser]

yacht	яхта	[jaχta]
tugboat	таноби ядак	[tanobi jadak]
barge	баржа	[barʒa]
ferry	паром	[parom]

| sailing ship | киштии бодбондор | [kiʃti:i bodbondor] |
| brigantine | бригантина | [brigantina] |

| ice breaker | киштии яхшикан | [kiʃti:i jaχʃikan] |
| submarine | киштии зериобӣ | [kiʃti:i zeriobi:] |

boat (flat-bottomed ~)	қаиқ	[qaiq]
dinghy	қаиқ	[qaiq]
lifeboat	заврақи наҷот	[zavraqi nadʒot]
motorboat	катер	[kater]

captain	капитан	[kapitan]
seaman	баҳрчӣ, маллоҳ	[bahrtʃi:], [malloh]
sailor	баҳрчӣ	[bahrtʃi:]
crew	экипаж	[ɛkipaʒ]

boatswain	ботсман	[botsman]
ship's boy	маллоҳбача	[mallohbatʃa]
cook	кок, ошпази киштӣ	[kok], [oʃpazi kiʃti:]
ship's doctor	духтури киштӣ	[duχturi kiʃti:]

deck	саҳни киштӣ	[sahni kiʃti:]
mast	сутуни киштӣ	[sutuni kiʃti:]
sail	бодбон	[bodbon]
hold	таҳхонаи киштӣ	[tahχonai kiʃti:]
bow (prow)	сари кишти	[sari kiʃti]

stern	думи киштй	[dumi kiʃti:]
oar	бели завраҡ	[beli zavraq]
screw propeller	винт	[vint]
cabin	каюта	[kajuta]
wardroom	кают-компания	[kajut-kompanija]
engine room	шӯъбаи мошинхо	[ʃœ'bai moʃinho]
bridge	арша	[arʃa]
radio room	радиохона	[radioxona]
wave (radio)	мавч	[mavʤ]
logbook	журнали киштй	[ʒurnali kiʃti:]
spyglass	дурбин	[durbin]
bell	нохус, зангӯла	[noqus], [zangœla]
flag	байрак	[bajrak]
hawser (mooring ~)	арғамчини ғафс	[arʁamtʃini ʁafs]
knot (bowline, etc.)	гирех	[gireh]
deckrails	даста барои ҡапидан	[dasta baroi qapidan]
gangway	зинапоя	[zinapoja]
anchor	лангар	[langar]
to weigh anchor	лангар бардоштан	[langar bardoʃtan]
to drop anchor	лангар андохтан	[langar andoxtan]
anchor chain	занчири лангар	[zanʤiri langar]
port (harbor)	бандар	[bandar]
quay, wharf	чои киштибандй	[ʤoi kiʃtibandi:]
to berth (moor)	ба сохил овардан	[ba sohil ovardan]
to cast off	харакат кардан	[harakat kardan]
trip, voyage	саёхат	[sajɔhat]
cruise (sea trip)	круиз	[kruiz]
course (route)	самт	[samt]
route (itinerary)	маршрут	[marʃrut]
fairway (safe water channel)	маъбар	[ma'bar]
shallows	тунукоба	[tunukoba]
to run aground	ба тунукоба шиштан	[ba tunukoba ʃiʃtan]
storm	тӯфон, бӯрои	[tœfon], [bœroi]
signal	бонг, ишорат	[bong], [iʃorat]
to sink (vi)	ғарк шудан	[ʁark ʃudan]
Man overboard!	Одам дар об!	[odam dar ob]
SOS (distress signal)	SOS	[sos]
ring buoy	чамбари начот	[tʃambari naʤot]

CITY

T&P Books Publishing

bus	автобус	[avtobus]
streetcar	трамвай	[tramvaj]
trolley bus	троллейбус	[trollejbus]
route (of bus, etc.)	маршрут	[marʃrut]
number (e.g., bus ~)	рақам	[raqam]
to go by ...	савор будан	[savor budan]
to get on (~ the bus)	савор шудан	[savor ʃudan]
to get off ...	фуромадан	[furomadan]
stop (e.g., bus ~)	истгоҳ	[istgoh]
next stop	истгоҳи дигар	[istgohi digar]
terminus	истгоҳи охирон	[istgohi oχiron]
schedule	ҷадвал	[dʒadval]
to wait (vt)	поидан	[poidan]
ticket	билет	[bilet]
fare	арзиши чипта	[arziʃi tʃipta]
cashier (ticket seller)	кассир	[kassir]
ticket inspection	назорат	[nazorat]
ticket inspector	нозир	[nozir]
to be late (for ...)	дер мондан	[der mondan]
to miss (~ the train, etc.)	дер мондан	[der mondan]
to be in a hurry	шитоб кардан	[ʃitob kardan]
taxi, cab	такси	[taksi]
taxi driver	таксичӣ	[taksitʃi:]
by taxi	дар такси	[dar taksi]
taxi stand	истгоҳи таксӣ	[istgohi taksi:]
to call a taxi	даъват кардани таксӣ	[da'vat kardani taksi:]
to take a taxi	такси гирифтан	[taksi giriftan]
traffic	ҳаракат дар кӯча	[harakat dar kœtʃa]
traffic jam	пробка	[probka]
rush hour	час пик	[tʃas pik]
to park (vi)	ҷой кардан	[dʒoj kardan]
to park (vt)	ҷой кардан	[dʒoj kardan]
parking lot	истгоҳ	[istgoh]
subway	метро	[metro]
station	истгоҳ	[istgoh]
to take the subway	бо метро рафтан	[bo metro raftan]

| train | поезд, қатор | [poezd], [qator] |
| train station | вокзал | [vokzal] |

28. City. Life in the city

city, town	шаҳр	[ʃahr]
capital city	пойтахт	[pojtaχt]
village	деҳа, деҳ	[deha], [deh]

city map	нақшаи шаҳр	[naqʃai ʃahr]
downtown	маркази шаҳр	[markazi ʃahr]
suburb	шаҳрча	[ʃahrtʃa]
suburban (adj)	наздишаҳрӣ	[nazdiʃahri:]

outskirts	атроф, канор	[atrof], [kanor]
environs (suburbs)	атрофи шаҳр	[atrofi ʃahr]
city block	квартал, маҳалла	[kvartal], [mahalla]
residential block (area)	маҳаллаи истиқоматӣ	[mahallai istiqomati:]

traffic	ҳаракат дар кӯча	[harakat dar kœtʃa]
traffic lights	чароғи раҳнамо	[tʃaroʁi rahnamo]
public transportation	нақлиёти шаҳрӣ	[naqlijoti ʃahri:]
intersection	чорраҳа	[tʃorraha]

crosswalk	гузаргоҳи пиёдагардон	[guzargohi pijodagardon]
pedestrian underpass	гузаргоҳи зеризаминӣ	[guzargohi zerizamini:]
to cross (~ the street)	гузаштан	[guzaʃtan]
pedestrian	пиёдагард	[pijodagard]
sidewalk	пиёдараҳа	[pijodaraha]

bridge	пул, кӯпрук	[pul], [kœpruk]
embankment (river walk)	соҳил	[sohil]
fountain	фаввора	[favvora]

allée (garden walkway)	кӯчабоғ	[kœtʃaboʁ]
park	боғ	[boʁ]
boulevard	кӯчабоғ, гулгашт	[kœtʃaboʁ], [gulgaʃt]
square	майдон	[majdon]
avenue (wide street)	хиёбон	[χijobon]
street	кӯча	[kœtʃa]
side street	тангкӯча	[tangkœtʃa]
dead end	кӯчаи бумбаста	[kœtʃai bumbasta]

house	хона	[χona]
building	бино	[bino]
skyscraper	иморати осмонхарош	[imorati osmonχaroʃ]

facade	намо	[namo]
roof	бом	[bom]
window	тиреза	[tireza]

arch	равоқ, тоқ	[ravoq], [toq]
column	сутун	[sutun]
corner	бурчак	[burtʃak]

store window	витрина	[vitrina]
signboard (store sign, etc.)	лавҳа	[lavha]
poster	эълоннома	[ɛ'lonnoma]
advertising poster	плакати реклама	[plakati reklama]
billboard	лавҳаи эълонхо	[lavhai ɛ'lonho]

garbage, trash	ахлот, хокрӯба	[aχlot], [χokrœba]
trashcan (public ~)	ахлотқуттӣ	[aχlotqutti:]
to litter (vi)	ифлос кардан	[iflos kardan]
garbage dump	партовгоҳ	[partovgoh]

phone booth	будкаи телефон	[budkai telefon]
lamppost	сутуни фонус	[sutuni fonus]
bench (park ~)	нимкат	[nimkat]

police officer	полис	[polis]
police	полис	[polis]
beggar	гадо	[gado]
homeless (n)	бехона	[beχona]

29. Urban institutions

store	магазин	[magazin]
drugstore, pharmacy	дорухона	[doruχona]
eyeglass store	оптика	[optika]
shopping mall	маркази савдо	[markazi savdo]
supermarket	супермаркет	[supermarket]

bakery	дӯкони нонфурӯшӣ	[dœkoni nonfurœʃi:]
baker	нонвой	[nonvoj]
pastry shop	қаннодӣ	[qannodi:]
grocery store	дӯкони баққолӣ	[dœkoni baqqoli:]
butcher shop	дӯкони гӯштфурӯшӣ	[dœkoni gœʃtfurœʃi:]

| produce store | дӯкони сабзавот | [dœkoni sabzavot] |
| market | бозор | [bozor] |

coffee house	қаҳвахона	[qahvaχona]
restaurant	тарабхона	[tarabχona]
pub, bar	пивохона	[pivoχona]
pizzeria	питсерия	[pitserija]

hair salon	сартарошхона	[sartaroʃχona]
post office	пӯшта	[pœʃta]
dry cleaners	козургарии химиявӣ	[kozurgari:i χimijavi:]
photo studio	суратгирхона	[suratgirχona]

shoe store	магазини пойафзолфурӯшӣ	[magazini pojafzolfurœʃi:]
bookstore	мағозаи китоб	[maʁozai kitob]
sporting goods store	мағозаи варзишӣ	[maʁozai varziʃi:]
clothes repair shop	таъмири либос	[ta'miri libos]
formal wear rental	кирояи либос	[kirojai libos]
video rental store	кирояи филмхо	[kirojai filmho]
circus	сирк	[sirk]
zoo	боги хайвонот	[boʁi hajvonot]
movie theater	кинотеатр	[kinoteatr]
museum	осорхона	[osorχona]
library	китобхона	[kitobχona]
theater	театр	[teatr]
opera (opera house)	опера	[opera]
nightclub	клуби шабона	[klubi ʃabona]
casino	казино	[kazino]
mosque	масчид	[masdʒid]
synagogue	каниса	[kanisa]
cathedral	собор	[sobor]
temple	ибодатгох	[ibodatgoh]
church	калисо	[kaliso]
college	институт	[institut]
university	университет	[universitet]
school	мактаб	[maktab]
prefecture	префектура	[prefektura]
city hall	мэрия	[mɛrija]
hotel	мехмонхона	[mehmonχona]
bank	банк	[bank]
embassy	сафорат	[saforat]
travel agency	турагенство	[turagenstvo]
information office	бюрои справкадихӣ	[bjuroi spravkadihi:]
currency exchange	нуқтаи мубодила	[nuqtai mubodila]
subway	метро	[metro]
hospital	касалхона	[kasalχona]
gas station	нуқтаи фурӯши сӯзишворӣ	[nuqtai furœʃi sœziʃvori:]
parking lot	истгохи мошинхо	[istgohi moʃinho]

30. Signs

signboard (store sign, etc.)	лавха	[lavha]
notice (door sign, etc.)	хат, навиштачот	[χat], [naviʃtadʒot]

poster	плакат	[plakat]
direction sign	аломат, нишона	[alomat], [niʃona]
arrow (sign)	аломати тир	[alomati tir]

caution	огоҳӣ	[ogohi:]
warning sign	огоҳӣ	[ogohi:]
to warn (vt)	танбеҳ додан	[tanbeh dodan]

rest day (weekly ~)	рӯзи истироҳат	[rœzi istirohat]
timetable (schedule)	ҷадвал	[dʒadval]
opening hours	соати корӣ	[soati kori:]

WELCOME!	ХУШ ОМАДЕД!	[xuʃ omaded]
ENTRANCE	ДАРОМАД	[daromad]
EXIT	БАРОМАД	[baromad]

PUSH	АЗ ХУД	[az xud]
PULL	БА ХУД	[ba xud]
OPEN	КУШОДА	[kuʃoda]
CLOSED	ПӮШИДА	[pœʃida]

| WOMEN | БАРОИ ЗАНОН | [baroi zanon] |
| MEN | БАРОИ МАРДОН | [baroi mardon] |

DISCOUNTS	ТАХФИФ	[taxfif]
SALE	АРЗОНФУРӮШӢ	[arzonfurœʃi:]
NEW!	МОЛИ НАВ!	[moli nav]
FREE	БЕПУЛ	[bepul]

ATTENTION!	ДИҚҚАТ!	[diqqat]
NO VACANCIES	ҶОЙ НЕСТ	[dʒoj nest]
RESERVED	БАНД АСТ	[band ast]

| ADMINISTRATION | МАЪМУРИЯТ | [ma'murijat] |
| STAFF ONLY | ФАҚАТ БАРОИ КОРМАНДОН | [faqat baroi kormandon] |

BEWARE OF THE DOG!	САГИ ГАЗАНДА	[sagi gazanda]
NO SMOKING	ТАМОКУ НАКАШЕД!	[tamoku nakaʃed]
DO NOT TOUCH!	ДАСТ НАРАСОНЕД!	[dast narasoned]

DANGEROUS	ХАТАРНОК	[xatarnok]
DANGER	ХАТАР	[xatar]
HIGH VOLTAGE	ШИДДАТИ БАЛАНД	[ʃiddati baland]
NO SWIMMING!	ОББОЗӢ КАРДАН МАНЪ АСТ	[obbozi: kardan man' ast]
OUT OF ORDER	КОР НАМЕКУНАД	[kor namekunad]

FLAMMABLE	ОТАШАНГЕЗ	[otaʃangez]
FORBIDDEN	МАНЪ АСТ	[man' ast]
NO TRESPASSING!	ДАРОМАД МАНЪ АСТ	[daromad man' ast]
WET PAINT	РАНГ КАРДА ШУДААСТ	[rang karda ʃudaast]

31. Shopping

to buy (purchase)	харидан	[xaridan]
purchase	харид	[xarid]
to go shopping	харид кардан	[xarid kardan]
shopping	шопинг	[ʃoping]
to be open (ab. store)	кушода будан	[kuʃoda budan]
to be closed	маҳкам будан	[mahkam budan]
footwear, shoes	пойафзол	[pojafzol]
clothes, clothing	либос	[libos]
cosmetics	косметика	[kosmetika]
food products	озуқаворӣ	[ozuqavori:]
gift, present	тӯҳфа	[tœhfa]
salesman	фурӯш	[furœʃ]
saleswoman	фурӯш	[furœʃ]
check out, cash desk	касса	[kassa]
mirror	оина	[oina]
counter (store ~)	пешдӯкон	[peʃdœkon]
fitting room	ҷои пӯшида дидани либос	[dʒoi pœʃida didani libos]
to try on	пӯшида дидан	[pœʃida didan]
to fit (ab. dress, etc.)	мувофиқ омадан	[muvofiq omadan]
to like (I like …)	форидан	[foridan]
price	нарх	[narx]
price tag	нархнома	[narxnoma]
to cost (vt)	арзидан	[arzidan]
How much?	Чанд пул?	[tʃand pul]
discount	тахфиф	[taxfif]
inexpensive (adj)	арзон	[arzon]
cheap (adj)	арзон	[arzon]
expensive (adj)	қимат	[qimat]
It's expensive	Ин қимат аст	[in qimat ast]
rental (n)	кироя	[kiroja]
to rent (~ a tuxedo)	насия гирифтан	[nasija giriftan]
credit (trade credit)	қарз	[qarz]
on credit (adv)	кредит гирифтан	[kredit giriftan]

CLOTHING & ACCESSORIES

T&P Books Publishing

32. Outerwear. Coats

clothes	**либос**	[libos]
outerwear	**либоси боло**	[libosi bolo]
winter clothing	**либоси зимистонй**	[libosi zimistoni:]
coat (overcoat)	**палто**	[palto]
fur coat	**пӯстин**	[pœstin]
fur jacket	**нимпӯстин**	[nimpœstin]
down coat	**пуховик**	[puχovik]
jacket (e.g., leather ~)	**куртка**	[kurtka]
raincoat (trenchcoat, etc.)	**боронй**	[boroni:]
waterproof (adj)	**обногузар**	[obnoguzar]

33. Men's & women's clothing

shirt (button shirt)	**курта**	[kurta]
pants	**шим, шалвор**	[ʃim], [ʃalvor]
jeans	**шими ҷинс**	[ʃimi dʒins]
suit jacket	**пичак**	[pidʒak]
suit	**костюм**	[kostjum]
dress (frock)	**куртаи заннона**	[kurtai zannona]
skirt	**юбка**	[jubka]
blouse	**блузка**	[bluzka]
knitted jacket (cardigan, etc.)	**кофтаи бофта**	[koftai bofta]
jacket (of woman's suit)	**жакет**	[ʒaket]
T-shirt	**футболка**	[futbolka]
shorts (short trousers)	**шортик**	[ʃortik]
tracksuit	**либоси варзишй**	[libosi varziʃi:]
bathrobe	**халат**	[χalat]
pajamas	**пижама**	[piʒama]
sweater	**свитер**	[sviter]
pullover	**пуловер**	[pulover]
vest	**камзӯл**	[kamzœl]
tailcoat	**фрак**	[frak]
tuxedo	**смокинг**	[smoking]
uniform	**либоси расмй**	[libosi rasmi:]
workwear	**либоси корй**	[libosi kori:]

| overalls | комбинезон | [kombinezon] |
| coat (e.g., doctor's smock) | халат | [χalat] |

34. Clothing. Underwear

underwear	либоси таг	[libosi tag]
boxers, briefs	турсуки мардона	[tursuki mardona]
panties	турсуки занона	[tursuki zanona]
undershirt (A-shirt)	майка	[majka]
socks	пайпоқ	[pajpoq]

nightgown	куртаи хоб	[kurtai χob]
bra	синабанд	[sinaband]
knee highs (knee-high socks)	чуроби кутох	[dʒurobi kutoh]

pantyhose	колготка	[kolgotka]
stockings (thigh highs)	чуроби дароз	[tʃurobi daroz]
bathing suit	либоси оббозй	[libosi obbozi:]

35. Headwear

hat	кулох, телпак	[kuloh], [telpak]
fedora	шляпаи мохутй	[ʃljapai mohuti:]
baseball cap	бейсболка	[bejsbolka]
flatcap	кепка	[kepka]

beret	берет	[beret]
hood	либоси кулохдор	[libosi kulohdor]
panama hat	панамка	[panamka]
knit cap (knitted hat)	шапкаи бофтагй	[ʃapkai boftagi:]

| headscarf | рӯймол | [rœjmol] |
| women's hat | кулохча | [kulohtʃa] |

hard hat	тоскулох	[toskuloh]
garrison cap	пилотка	[pilotka]
helmet	хӯд	[χœd]

| derby | дегчакулох | [degtʃakuloχ] |
| top hat | силиндр | [silindr] |

36. Footwear

footwear	пойафзол	[pojafzol]
shoes (men's shoes)	патинка	[patinka]
shoes (women's shoes)	кафш, туфли	[kafʃ], [tufli]

boots (e.g., cowboy ~)	мӯза	[mœza]
slippers	шиппак	[ʃippak]
tennis shoes (e.g., Nike ~)	крассовка	[krassovka]
sneakers (e.g., Converse ~)	кетӣ	[keti:]
sandals	сандал	[sandal]
cobbler (shoe repairer)	мӯзадӯз	[mœzadœz]
heel	пошна	[poʃna]
pair (of shoes)	чуфт	[dʒuft]
shoestring	бандак	[bandak]
to lace (vt)	бандак гузарондан	[bandak guzarondan]
shoehorn	кафчаи кафшпӯшӣ	[kaftʃai kafʃpœʃi:]
shoe polish	креми пойафзол	[kremi pojafzol]

37. Personal accessories

gloves	дастпӯшак	[dastpœʃak]
mittens	дастпӯшаки бепанҷа	[dastpœʃaki bepandʒa]
scarf (muffler)	гарданпеч	[gardanpetʃ]
glasses (eyeglasses)	айнак	[ajnak]
frame (eyeglass ~)	чанбарак	[tʃanbarak]
umbrella	соябон, чатр	[sojabon], [tʃatr]
walking stick	чӯб	[tʃœb]
hairbrush	чӯткаи мӯйсар	[tʃœtkai mœjsar]
fan	бодбезак	[bodbezak]
tie (necktie)	галстук	[galstuk]
bow tie	галстук-шапарак	[galstuk-ʃaparak]
suspenders	шалворбанди китфӣ	[ʃalvorbandi kitfi:]
handkerchief	дастрӯймол	[dastrœjmol]
comb	шона	[ʃona]
barrette	сарсӯзан, бандак	[sarsœzan], [bandak]
hairpin	санҷак	[sandʒak]
buckle	сагаки тасма	[sagaki tasma]
belt	тасма	[tasma]
shoulder strap	тасма	[tasma]
bag (handbag)	сумка	[sumka]
purse	сумка	[sumka]
backpack	борхалта	[borxalta]

38. Clothing. Miscellaneous

fashion	мод	[mod]
in vogue (adj)	модшуда	[modʃuda]
fashion designer	тархсоз	[tarhsoz]

collar	гиребон, ёқа	[girebon], [jɔqa]
pocket	киса	[kisa]
pocket (as adj)	... и киса	[i kisa]
sleeve	остин	[ostin]
hanging loop	банди либос	[bandi libos]
fly (on trousers)	чоки пеши шим	[tʃoki peʃi ʃim]

zipper (fastener)	занчирак	[zandʒirak]
fastener	гиреҳбанд	[girehband]
button	тугма	[tugma]
buttonhole	банди тугма	[bandi tugma]
to come off (ab. button)	канда шудан	[kanda ʃudan]

to sew (vi, vt)	дӯхтан	[dœxtan]
to embroider (vi, vt)	гулдӯзи кардан	[guldœzi: kardan]
embroidery	гулдӯзи	[guldœzi:]
sewing needle	сӯзани чокдӯзи	[sœzani tʃokdœzi]
thread	ресмон	[resmon]
seam	чок	[tʃok]

to get dirty (vi)	олуда шудан	[oluda ʃudan]
stain (mark, spot)	доғ, лакка	[doʁ], [lakka]
to crease, crumple (vi)	ғичим шудан	[ʁidʒim ʃudan]
to tear, to rip (vt)	даррондан	[darrondan]
clothes moth	куя	[kuja]

39. Personal care. Cosmetics

toothpaste	хамираи дандон	[xamirai dandon]
toothbrush	чӯткаи дандоншӯй	[tʃœtkai dandonʃœi:]
to brush one's teeth	дандон шустан	[dandon ʃustan]

razor	ришгирак	[riʃgirak]
shaving cream	креми ришгири	[kremi riʃgiri:]
to shave (vi)	риш гирифтан	[riʃ giriftan]

soap	собун	[sobun]
shampoo	шампун	[ʃampun]

scissors	кайчи	[kajtʃi:]
nail file	тарошаи нохунхо	[taroʃai noxunho]
nail clippers	анбӯрча барои нохунхо	[anbœrtʃa baroi noxunho]
tweezers	мӯйчинак	[mœjtʃinak]

cosmetics	косметика	[kosmetika]
face mask	ниқоби косметикӣ	[niqobi kosmetiki:]
manicure	нохунорой	[noχunoroi:]
to have a manicure	нохун оростан	[noχun orostan]
pedicure	ороиши нохунхои пой	[oroiʃi noχunhoi poj]

make-up bag	косметичка	[kosmetitʃka]
face powder	сафеда	[safeda]
powder compact	қуттии упо	[qutti:i upo]
blusher	сурхӣ	[surχi:]

toilet water (lotion)	атр	[atr]
lotion	оби мушкин	[obi muʃkin]
cologne	атр	[atr]

eyeshadow	тен барои пилкхои чашм	[ten baroi pilkhoi tʃaʃm]
eyeliner	қалами чашм	[qalami tʃaʃm]
mascara	туш барои мижахо	[tuʃ baroi miʒaho]

lipstick	лабсурхкунак	[labsurχkunak]
nail polish, enamel	лаки нохун	[laki noχun]
hair spray	лаки мӯйсар	[laki mœjsar]
deodorant	дезодорант	[dezodorant]

cream	крем, равгани рӯй	[krem], [ravɐani rœj]
face cream	креми рӯй	[kremi rœj]
hand cream	креми даст	[kremi dast]
anti-wrinkle cream	креми зиддиожанг	[kremi ziddioʒang]
day cream	креми рӯзона	[kremi rœzona]
night cream	креми шабона	[kremi ʃabona]
day (as adj)	рӯзона, ~и рӯз	[rœzona], [~i rœz]
night (as adj)	шабона, … и шаб	[ʃabona], [i ʃab]

tampon	тампон	[tampon]
toilet paper (toilet roll)	когази хоҷатхона	[koɐazi χoʤatχona]
hair dryer	мӯхушккунак	[mœχuʃkkunak]

40. Watches. Clocks

watch (wristwatch)	соати дастӣ	[soati dasti:]
dial	лавхаи соат	[lavhai soat]
hand (of clock, watch)	акрабак	[akrabak]
metal watch band	дастпона	[dastpona]
watch strap	банди соат	[bandi soat]

battery	батареяча, батарейка	[batarejatʃa], [batarejka]
to be dead (battery)	холӣ шудааст	[χoli: ʃudaast]
to change a battery	иваз кардани батаре	[ivaz kardani batare]
to run fast	пеш меравад	[peʃ meravad]

to run slow	ақиб мондан	[aqib mondan]
wall clock	соати деворй	[soati devori:]
hourglass	соати регй	[soati regi:]
sundial	соати офтобй	[soati oftobi:]
alarm clock	соати рӯимизии зангдор	[soati rœimizi:i zangdor]
watchmaker	соатсоз	[soatsoz]
to repair (vt)	таъмир кардан	[ta'mir kardan]

EVERYDAY EXPERIENCE

T&P Books Publishing

41. Money

money	пул	[pul]
currency exchange	мубодила, иваз	[mubodila], [ivaz]
exchange rate	курб	[qurb]
ATM	банкомат	[bankomat]
coin	танга	[tanga]

dollar	доллар	[dollar]
lira	лираи италиявӣ	[lirai italijavi:]
Deutschmark	маркаи олмонӣ	[markai olmoni:]
franc	франк	[frank]
pound sterling	фунт стерлинг	[funt sterling]
yen	иена	[iena]

debt	қарз	[qarz]
debtor	қарздор	[qarzdor]
to lend (money)	қарз додан	[qarz dodan]
to borrow (vi, vt)	қарз гирифтан	[qarz giriftan]

bank	банк	[bank]
account	ҳисоб	[hisob]
to deposit (vt)	гузарондан	[guzarondan]
to deposit into the account	ба суратҳисоб гузарондан	[ba surathisob guzarondan]
to withdraw (vt)	аз суратҳисоб гирифтан	[az surathisob giriftan]

credit card	корти кредитӣ	[korti krediti:]
cash	пули нақд, нақдина	[puli naqd], [naqdina]
check	чек	[tʃek]
to write a check	чек навиштан	[tʃek naviʃtan]
checkbook	дафтарчаи чек	[daftartʃai tʃek]

wallet	ҳамён	[hamjɔn]
change purse	ҳамён	[hamjɔn]
safe	сейф	[sejf]

heir	меросхӯр	[merosχœr]
inheritance	мерос	[meros]
fortune (wealth)	дорой	[doroi:]

lease	иҷора	[idʒora]
rent (money)	ҳаққи манзил	[haqqi manzil]
to rent (sth from sb)	ба иҷора гирифтан	[ba idʒora giriftan]
price	нарх	[narχ]

cost	арзиш	[arziʃ]
sum	маблағ	[mablaʁ]
to spend (vt)	сарф кардан	[sarf kardan]
expenses	харч, ҳазина	[xardʒ], [hazina]
to economize (vi, vt)	сарфа кардан	[sarfa kardan]
economical	сарфакор	[sarfakor]
to pay (vi, vt)	пул додан	[pul dodan]
payment	пардохт	[pardoχt]
change (give the ~)	бақияи пул	[baqijai pul]
tax	налог, андоз	[nalog], [andoz]
fine	чарима	[dʒarima]
to fine (vt)	чарима андохтан	[dʒarima andoχtan]

42. Post. Postal service

post office	почта	[potʃta]
mail (letters, etc.)	почта	[potʃta]
mailman	хаткашон	[χatkaʃon]
opening hours	соати корӣ	[soati kori:]
letter	мактуб	[maktub]
registered letter	хати супоришӣ	[χati suporiʃi:]
postcard	рукъа	[ruq'a]
telegram	барқия	[barqija]
package (parcel)	равонак	[ravonak]
money transfer	пули фиристодашуда	[puli firistodaʃuda]
to receive (vt)	гирифтан	[giriftan]
to send (vt)	ирсол кардан	[irsol kardan]
sending	ирсол	[irsol]
address	адрес, унвон	[adres], [unvon]
ZIP code	индекси почта	[indeksi potʃta]
sender	ирсолкунанда	[irsolkunanda]
receiver	гиранда	[giranda]
name (first name)	ном	[nom]
surname (last name)	фамилия	[familija]
postage rate	таърифа	[ta'rifa]
standard (adj)	муқаррарӣ	[muqarrari:]
economical (adj)	камхарч	[kamχardʒ]
weight	вазн	[vazn]
to weigh (~ letters)	баркашидан	[barkaʃidan]
envelope	конверт	[konvert]
postage stamp	марка	[marka]
to stamp an envelope	марка часпонидан	[marka tʃasponidan]

43. Banking

bank	банк	[bank]
branch (of bank, etc.)	шӯъба	[ʃœ'ba]
bank clerk, consultant	мушовир	[muʃovir]
manager (director)	идоракунанда	[idorakunanda]
bank account	ҳисоб	[hisob]
account number	рақами суратҳисоб	[raqami surathisob]
checking account	ҳисоби ҷорӣ	[hisobi dʒori:]
savings account	суратҳисоби	[surathisobi
	ҷамъшаванда	dʒam'ʃavanda]
to open an account	суратҳисоб кушодан	[surathisob kuʃodan]
to close the account	бастани суратҳисоб	[bastani surathisob]
to deposit into the account	ба суратҳисоб	[ba surathisob
	гузарондан	guzarondan]
to withdraw (vt)	аз суратҳисоб	[az surathisob
	гирифтан	giriftan]
deposit	амонат	[amonat]
to make a deposit	маблағ гузоштан	[mablaʁ guzoʃtan]
wire transfer	интиқоли маблағ	[intiqoli mablaʁ]
to wire, to transfer	интиқол додан	[intiqol dodan]
sum	маблағ	[mablaʁ]
How much?	Чӣ қадар?	[tʃi: qadar]
signature	имзо	[imzo]
to sign (vt)	имзо кардан	[imzo kardan]
credit card	корти кредитӣ	[korti krediti:]
code (PIN code)	рамз, код	[ramz], [kod]
credit card number	рақами корти кредитӣ	[raqami korti krediti:]
ATM	банкомат	[bankomat]
check	чек	[tʃek]
to write a check	чек навиштан	[tʃek naviʃtan]
checkbook	дафтарчаи чек	[daftartʃai tʃek]
loan (bank ~)	қарз	[qarz]
to apply for a loan	барои кредит	[baroi kredit
	муроҷиат кардан	murodʒiat kardan]
to get a loan	кредит гирифтан	[kredit giriftan]
to give a loan	кредит додан	[kredit dodan]
guarantee	кафолат, замонат	[kafolat], [zamonat]

44. Telephone. Phone conversation

telephone	телефон	[telefon]
cell phone	телефони мобилй	[telefoni mobili:]
answering machine	худчавобгӯ	[xuddʒavobgœ]
to call (by phone)	телефон кардан	[telefon kardan]
phone call	занг	[zang]
to dial a number	гирифтани рақамхо	[giriftani raqamho]
Hello!	алло, ҳа	[allo], [ha]
to ask (vt)	пурсидан	[pursidan]
to answer (vi, vt)	чавоб додан	[dʒavob dodan]
to hear (vt)	шунидан	[ʃunidan]
well (adv)	хуб, наӻз	[xub], [naɞz]
not well (adv)	бад	[bad]
noises (interference)	садохои бегона	[sadohoi begona]
receiver	гӯшак	[giːʃak]
to pick up (~ the phone)	бардоштани гӯшак	[bardoʃtani gœʃak]
to hang up (~ the phone)	мондани гӯшак	[mondani gœʃak]
busy (engaged)	банд	[band]
to ring (ab. phone)	занг задан	[zang zadan]
telephone book	китоби телефон	[kitobi telefon]
local (adj)	маҳаллй	[mahalli:]
local call	занги маҳаллй	[zangi mahalli:]
long distance (~ call)	байнишаҳрй	[bajniʃahri:]
long-distance call	занги байнишаҳрй	[zangi bajniʃahri:]
international (adj)	байналхалқй	[bajnalxalqi:]

45. Cell phone

cell phone	телефони мобилй	[telefoni mobili:]
display	дисплей	[displej]
button	тугмача	[tugmatʃa]
SIM card	сим-корт	[sim-kort]
battery	батарея	[batareja]
to be dead (battery)	бе заряд шудан	[be zarjad ʃudan]
charger	асбоби барқпуркунанда	[asbobi barqpurkunanda]
menu	меню	[menju]
settings	соз кардан	[soz kardan]
tune (melody)	оҳанг	[ohang]
to select (vt)	интихоб кардан	[intixob kardan]
calculator	ҳисобкунак	[hisobkunak]

voice mail	худчавобгӯ	[xudʤavobgœ]
alarm clock	соати рӯимизии зангдор	[soati rœimizi:i zangdor]
contacts	китоби телефон	[kitobi telefon]

| SMS (text message) | СМС-хабар | [sms-xabar] |
| subscriber | муштарй | [muʃtari:] |

46. Stationery

| ballpoint pen | ручкаи саққочадор | [rutʃkai saqqotʃador] |
| fountain pen | парқалам | [parqalam] |

pencil	қалам	[qalam]
highlighter	маркер	[marker]
felt-tip pen	фломастер	[flomaster]

| notepad | блокнот, дафтари ёддошт | [bloknot], [daftari jòddoʃt] |
| agenda (diary) | рӯзнома | [rœznoma] |

ruler	чадвал	[ʤadval]
calculator	ҳисобкунак	[hisobkunak]
eraser	ластик	[lastik]
thumbtack	кнопка	[knopka]
paper clip	скрепка	[skrepka]

glue	елим, шилм	[elim], [ʃilm]
stapler	степлер	[stepler]
pencil sharpener	чарх	[tʃarx]

47. Foreign languages

language	забон	[zabon]
foreign (adj)	хоричй	[xoriʤi:]
foreign language	забони хоричй	[zaboni xoriʤi:]
to study (vt)	омӯхтан	[omœxtan]
to learn (language, etc.)	омӯхтан	[omœxtan]

to read (vi, vt)	хондан	[xondan]
to speak (vi, vt)	гап задан	[gap zadan]
to understand (vt)	фаҳмидан	[fahmidan]
to write (vt)	навиштан	[naviʃtan]

fast (adv)	босуръат	[bosur'at]
slowly (adv)	оҳиста	[ohista]
fluently (adv)	озодона	[ozodona]
rules	қоидаҳо	[qoidaho]

grammar	грамматика	[grammatika]
vocabulary	лексика	[leksika]
phonetics	савтиёт	[savtijɔt]

textbook	китоби дарсӣ	[kitobi darsi:]
dictionary	луғат	[luʁat]
teach-yourself book	худомӯз	[χudomœz]
phrasebook	сӯхбатнома	[sœhbatnoma]

cassette, tape	кассета	[kasseta]
videotape	видеокассета	[videokasseta]
CD, compact disc	CD, диски компактӣ	[ɔɛ], [diski kompakti:]
DVD	DVD-диск	[ɛøɛ-disk]

alphabet	алифбо	[alifbo]
to spell (vt)	ҳарфакӣ гап задан	[harfaki: gap zadan]
pronunciation	талаффуз	[talaffuz]

accent	зада, аксент	[zada], [aksent]
with an accent	бо аксент	[bo aksent]
without an accent	бе аксент	[be aksent]

| word | калима | [kalima] |
| meaning | маънӣ, маъно | [ma'ni:], [ma'no] |

course (e.g., a French ~)	курсҳо, дарсҳо	[kursho], [darsho]
to sign up	дохил шудан	[doχil ʃudan]
teacher	муаллим	[muallim]

translation (process)	тарҷума	[tardʒuma]
translation (text, etc.)	тарҷума	[tardʒuma]
translator	тарҷумон	[tardʒumon]
interpreter	тарҷумон	[tardʒumon]

| polyglot | забондон | [zabondon] |
| memory | ҳофиза | [hofiza] |

MEALS. RESTAURANT

T&P Books Publishing

48. Table setting

spoon	қошуқ	[qoʃuq]
knife	корд	[kord]
fork	чангча, чангол	[ʧangʧa], [ʧangol]

cup (e.g., coffee ~)	косача	[kosatʃa]
plate (dinner ~)	тақсимча	[taqsimʧa]
saucer	тақсимӣ, тақсимича	[taqsimi:], [taqsimitʃa]
napkin (on table)	салфетка	[salfetka]
toothpick	дандонковак	[dandonkovak]

49. Restaurant

restaurant	тарабхона	[tarabχona]
coffee house	қаҳвахона	[qahvaχona]
pub, bar	бар	[bar]
tearoom	чойхона	[ʧojχona]

waiter	пешхизмат	[peʃχizmat]
waitress	пешхизмат	[peʃχizmat]
bartender	бармен	[barmen]
menu	меню	[menju]
wine list	рӯйхати шаробҳо	[rœjχati ʃarobho]
to book a table	банд кардани миз	[band kardani miz]

course, dish	таом	[taom]
to order (meal)	супориш додан	[suporiʃ dodan]
to make an order	фармоиш додан	[farmoiʃ dodan]
aperitif	аперитив	[aperitiv]
appetizer	хӯриш, газак	[χœriʃ], [gazak]
dessert	десерт	[desert]

check	ҳисоб	[hisob]
to pay the check	пардохт кардан	[pardoχt kardan]
to give change	бақия додан	[baqija dodan]
tip	чойпулӣ	[ʧojpuli:]

50. Meals

food	хӯрок, таом	[χœrok], [taom]
to eat (vi, vt)	хӯрдан	[χœrdan]

breakfast	ноништа	[noniʃta]
to have breakfast	ноништа кардан	[noniʃta kardan]
lunch	хӯроки пешин	[χœroki peʃin]
to have lunch	хӯроки пешин хӯрдан	[χœroki peʃin χœrdan]
dinner	шом	[ʃom]
to have dinner	хӯроки шом хӯрдан	[χœroki ʃom χœrdan]

appetite	иштихо	[iʃtiho]
Enjoy your meal!	ош шавад!	[oʃ ʃavad]

to open (~ a bottle)	кушодан	[kuʃodan]
to spill (liquid)	резондан	[rezondan]
to spill out (vi)	рехтан	[reχtan]

to boil (vi)	ҷӯшидан	[dʒœʃidan]
to boil (vt)	ҷӯшондан	[dʒœʃondan]
boiled (~ water)	ҷӯшомада	[dʒœʃomada]
to chill, cool down (vt)	хунук кардан	[χunuk kardan]
to chill (vi)	хунук шудан	[χunuk ʃudan]

taste, flavor	маза, таъм	[maza], [ta'm]
aftertaste	таъм	[ta'm]

to slim down (lose weight)	хароб шудан	[χarob ʃudan]
diet	диета	[dieta]
vitamin	витамин	[vitamin]
calorie	калория	[kalorija]
vegetarian (n)	гӯштнахӯранда	[gœʃtnaχœranda]
vegetarian (adj)	бегӯшт	[begœʃt]

fats (nutrient)	равған	[ravʁan]
proteins	сафедаҳо	[safedaho]
carbohydrates	карбогидратҳо	[karbogidratho]

slice (of lemon, ham)	тилим, порча	[tilim], [portʃa]
piece (of cake, pie)	порча	[portʃa]
crumb	резгӣ	[rezgi:]
(of bread, cake, etc.)		

51. Cooked dishes

course, dish	таом	[taom]
cuisine	таомҳо	[taomho]
recipe	ретсепт	[retsept]
portion	навола	[navola]

salad	салат	[salat]
soup	шӯрбо	[ʃœrbo]
clear soup (broth)	булён	[buljɔn]
sandwich (bread)	бутерброд	[buterbrod]

fried eggs	тухмбирён	[tuχmbirjɔn]
hamburger (beefburger)	гамбургер	[gamburger]
beefsteak	бифштекс	[bifʃteks]

side dish	хӯриши таом	[χœriʃi taom]
spaghetti	спагеттӣ	[spagetti:]
mashed potatoes	пюре	[pjure]
pizza	питса	[pitsa]
porridge (oatmeal, etc.)	шӯла	[ʃœla]
omelet	омлет, тухмбирён	[omlet], [tuχmbirjɔn]

boiled (e.g., ~ beef)	чӯшондашуда	[ʤœʃondaʃuda]
smoked (adj)	дудхӯрда	[dudχœrda]
fried (adj)	бирён	[birjɔn]
dried (adj)	хушк	[χuʃk]
frozen (adj)	яхкарда	[jaχkarda]
pickled (adj)	дар сирко	[dar sirko
	хобондашуда	χobondaʃuda]

sweet (sugary)	ширин	[ʃirin]
salty (adj)	шӯр	[ʃœr]
cold (adj)	хунук	[χunuk]
hot (adj)	гарм	[garm]
bitter (adj)	талх	[talχ]
tasty (adj)	бомаза	[bomaza]

to cook in boiling water	пухтан, чӯшондан	[puχtan], [ʤœʃondan]
to cook (dinner)	пухтан	[puχtan]
to fry (vt)	бирён кардан	[birjɔn kardan]
to heat up (food)	гарм кардан	[garm kardan]

to salt (vt)	намак андохтан	[namak andoχtan]
to pepper (vt)	қаламфур андохтан	[qalamfur andoχtan]
to grate (vt)	тарошидан	[taroʃidan]
peel (n)	пӯст	[pœst]
to peel (vt)	пӯст кандан	[pœst kandan]

52. Food

meat	гӯшт	[gœʃt]
chicken	мурғ	[murʁ]
Rock Cornish hen (poussin)	чӯча	[tʃœʤa]
duck	мурғобӣ	[murʁobi:]
goose	қоз, ғоз	[qoz], [ʁoz]
game	сайди шикор	[sajdi ʃikor]
turkey	мурғи марчон	[murʁi marʤon]
pork	гӯшти хук	[gœʃti χuk]
veal	гӯшти гӯсола	[gœʃti gœsola]

lamb	гӯшти гӯсфанд	[gœʃti gœsfand]
beef	гӯшти гов	[gœʃti gov]
rabbit	харгӯш	[xargœʃ]

sausage (bologna, pepperoni, etc.)	ҳасиб	[hasib]
vienna sausage (frankfurter)	ҳасибча	[hasibtʃa]
bacon	бекон	[bekon]
ham	ветчина	[vettʃina]
gammon	рон	[ron]

pâté	паштет	[paʃtet]
liver	ҷигар	[dʒigar]
hamburger (ground beef)	гӯшти кӯфта	[gœʃti kœfta]
tongue	забон	[zabon]

egg	тухм	[tuxm]
eggs	тухм	[tuxm]
egg white	сафедии тухм	[safedi:i tuxm]
egg yolk	зардии тухм	[zardi:i tuxm]

fish	моҳӣ	[mohi:]
seafood	маҳсулоти баҳрӣ	[mahsuloti bahri:]
crustaceans	буғумпойҳо	[buʁumpojho]
caviar	тухми моҳӣ	[tuxmi mohi:]

crab	харчанг	[xartʃang]
shrimp	креветка	[krevetka]
oyster	садафак	[sadafak]
spiny lobster	лангуст	[langust]
octopus	ҳаштпо	[haʃtpo]
squid	калмар	[kalmar]

sturgeon	гӯшти тосмоҳӣ	[gœʃti tosmohi:]
salmon	озодмоҳӣ	[ozodmohi:]
halibut	палтус	[paltus]

cod	равғанмоҳӣ	[ravʁanmohi:]
mackerel	загӯтамоҳӣ	[zaʁœtamohi:]
tuna	самак	[samak]
eel	мормоҳӣ	[mormohi:]

trout	гулмоҳӣ	[gulmohi:]
sardine	саморис	[samoris]
pike	шӯртан	[ʃœrtan]
herring	шӯрмоҳӣ	[ʃœrmohi:]

bread	нон	[non]
cheese	панир	[panir]
sugar	шакар	[ʃakar]
salt	намак	[namak]

rice	биринҷ	[birindʒ]
pasta (macaroni)	макарон	[makaron]
noodles	угро	[ugro]

butter	равғани маска	[ravɻani maska]
vegetable oil	равғани пок	[ravɻani pok]
sunflower oil	равғани офтобпараст	[ravɻani oftobparast]
margarine	маргарин	[margarin]

| olives | зайтун | [zajtun] |
| olive oil | равғани зайтун | [ravɻani zajtun] |

milk	шир	[ʃir]
condensed milk	ширқиём	[ʃirqijɔm]
yogurt	йогурт	[jɔgurt]
sour cream	қаймок	[qajmok]
cream (of milk)	қаймоқ	[qajmoq]

| mayonnaise | майонез | [majɔnez] |
| buttercream | крем | [krem] |

cereal grains (wheat, etc.)	ярма	[jarma]
flour	орд	[ord]
canned food	консерв	[konserv]

cornflakes	бадроқи чуворимакка	[badroqi dʒuvorimakka]
honey	асал	[asal]
jam	чем	[dʒem]
chewing gum	сақич, илқ	[saqitʃ], [ilq]

53. Drinks

water	об	[ob]
drinking water	оби нӯшиданӣ	[obi nœʃidani:]
mineral water	оби минералӣ	[obi minerali:]

still (adj)	бе газ	[be gaz]
carbonated (adj)	газнок	[gaznok]
sparkling (adj)	газдор	[gazdor]
ice	ях	[jaχ]
with ice	бо ях, яхдор	[bo jaχ], [jaχdor]

non-alcoholic (adj)	беалкогол	[bealkogol]
soft drink	нӯшокии беалкогол	[nœʃoki:i bealkogol]
refreshing drink	нӯшокии хунук	[nœʃoki:i χunuk]
lemonade	лимонад	[limonad]

liquors	нӯшокиҳои спиртӣ	[nœʃokihoi spirti:]
wine	шароб, май	[ʃarob], [maj]
white wine	маи ангури сафед	[mai anguri safed]

red wine	маи аргувонӣ	[mai arʁuvoni:]
liqueur	ликёр	[likjɔr]
champagne	шампан	[ʃampan]
vermouth	вермут	[vermut]

whiskey	виски	[viski]
vodka	арақ, водка	[araq], [vodka]
gin	чин	[dʒin]
cognac	коняк	[konjak]
rum	ром	[rom]

coffee	қаҳва	[qahva]
black coffee	қаҳваи сиёҳ	[qahvai sijɔh]
coffee with milk	ширқаҳва	[ʃirqahva]
cappuccino	капучино	[kaputʃino]
instant coffee	қаҳваи кӯфта	[qahvai kœfta]

milk	шир	[ʃir]
cocktail	коктейл	[koktejl]
milkshake	коктейли ширӣ	[koktejli ʃiri:]

juice	шарбат	[ʃarbat]
tomato juice	шираи помидор	[ʃirai pomidor]
orange juice	афшураи афлесун	[afʃurai aflesun]
freshly squeezed juice	афшураи тоза тайёршуда	[afʃurai toza tajjorʃuda]

beer	пиво	[pivo]
light beer	оби ҷави шафоф	[obi dʒavi ʃafof]
dark beer	оби ҷави торик	[obi dʒavi torik]

tea	чой	[tʃoj]
black tea	чойи сиёҳ	[tʃoji sijɔh]
green tea	чои кабуд	[tʃoi kabud]

54. Vegetables

| vegetables | сабзавот | [sabzavot] |
| greens | сабзавот | [sabzavot] |

tomato	помидор	[pomidor]
cucumber	бодиринг	[bodiring]
carrot	сабзӣ	[sabzi:]
potato	картошка	[kartoʃka]
onion	пиёз	[pijɔz]
garlic	сир	[sir]

cabbage	карам	[karam]
cauliflower	гулкарам	[gulkaram]
Brussels sprouts	карами брусселӣ	[karami brusseli:]

broccoli	карами брокколӣ	[karami brokkoli:]
beetroot	лаблабу	[lablabu]
eggplant	бодинҷон	[bodindʒon]
zucchini	таррак	[tarrak]
pumpkin	каду	[kadu]
turnip	шалғам	[ʃalʁam]

parsley	чаъфарӣ	[dʒa'fari:]
dill	шибит	[ʃibit]
lettuce	коху	[kohu]
celery	карафс	[karafs]
asparagus	морчӯба	[mortʃœba]
spinach	испаноқ	[ispanoq]

pea	нахӯд	[naχœd]
beans	лӯбиё	[lœbijɔ]
corn (maize)	чуворимакка	[dʒuvorimakka]
kidney bean	лӯбиё	[lœbijɔ]

bell pepper	қаламфур	[qalamfur]
radish	шалғамча	[ʃalʁamtʃa]
artichoke	анганор	[anganor]

55. Fruits. Nuts

fruit	мева	[meva]
apple	себ	[seb]
pear	мурӯд, нок	[murœd], [nok]
lemon	лиму	[limu]
orange	афлесун, пӯртахол	[aflesun], [pœrtaχol]
strawberry (garden ~)	қулфинай	[qulfinaj]

mandarin	норанг	[norang]
plum	олу	[olu]
peach	шафтолу	[ʃaftolu]
apricot	дарахти зардолу	[daraχti zardolu]
raspberry	тамашк	[tamaʃk]
pineapple	ананас	[ananas]

banana	банан	[banan]
watermelon	тарбуз	[tarbuz]
grape	ангур	[angur]
sour cherry	олуболу	[olubolu]
sweet cherry	гелос	[gelos]

grapefruit	норинҷ	[norindʒ]
avocado	авокадо	[avokado]
papaya	папайя	[papajja]
mango	анбах	[anbah]
pomegranate	анор	[anor]

redcurrant	коти сурх	[koti surχ]
blackcurrant	қоти сиёҳ	[qoti sijɔh]
gooseberry	бектошй	[bektoʃiː]
bilberry	черника	[tʃernika]
blackberry	марминҷон	[marmindʒon]

raisin	мавиз	[maviz]
fig	анҷир	[andʒir]
date	хурмо	[χurmo]

peanut	финдуки заминй	[finduki zamini:]
almond	бодом	[bodom]
walnut	чормағз	[tʃormaʁz]
hazelnut	финдиқ	[findiq]
coconut	норгил	[norgil]
pistachios	писта	[pista]

56. Bread. Candy

bakers' confectionery (pastry)	маҳсулоти қанноди	[mahsuloti qannodi]
bread	нон	[non]
cookies	кулчақанд	[kultʃaqand]

chocolate (n)	шоколад	[ʃokolad]
chocolate (as adj)	... и шоколад, шоколадй	[i ʃokolad], [ʃokoladiː]
candy (wrapped)	конфет	[konfet]
cake (e.g., cupcake)	пирожни	[pirɔʒni]
cake (e.g., birthday ~)	торт	[tort]

| pie (e.g., apple ~) | пирог | [pirog] |
| filling (for cake, pie) | пур кардани, андохтани | [pur kardani], [andɔχtani] |

jam (whole fruit jam)	мураббо	[murabbo]
marmalade	мармалод	[marmalod]
waffles	вафлй	[vafliː]
ice-cream	яхмос	[jaχmos]
pudding	пудинг	[puding]

57. Spices

salt	намак	[namak]
salty (adj)	шӯр	[ʃœr]
to salt (vt)	намак андохтан	[namak andɔχtan]

| black pepper | мурчи сиёҳ | [murtʃi sijɔh] |
| red pepper (milled ~) | мурчи сурх | [murtʃi surχ] |

mustard	хардал	[χardal]
horseradish	қаҳзак	[qahzak]
condiment	хӯриш	[χœriʃ]
spice	дорувор	[doruvor]
sauce	қайла	[qajla]
vinegar	сирко	[sirko]
anise	тухми бодиён	[tuχmi bodijɔn]
basil	нозбӯй, райҳон	[nozbœj], [rajhon]
cloves	қаланфури гардан	[qalanfuri gardan]
ginger	занҷабил	[zandʒabil]
coriander	кашнич	[kaʃnidʒ]
cinnamon	дорчин, долчин	[dortʃin], [doltʃin]
sesame	кунҷид	[kundʒid]
bay leaf	барги ғор	[bargi ʁor]
paprika	қаламфур	[qalamfur]
caraway	зира	[zira]
saffron	заъфарон	[za'faron]

PERSONAL
INFORMATION. FAMILY

T&P Books Publishing

58. Personal information. Forms

name (first name)	ном	[nom]
surname (last name)	фамилия	[familija]
date of birth	рӯзи таваллуд	[rœzi tavallud]
place of birth	ҷойи таваллуд	[dʒoji tavallud]
nationality	миллият	[millijat]
place of residence	ҷои истиқомат	[dʒoi istiqomat]
country	кишвар	[kiʃvar]
profession (occupation)	касб	[kasb]
gender, sex	ҷинс	[dʒins]
height	қад	[qad]
weight	вазн	[vazn]

59. Family members. Relatives

mother	модар	[modar]
father	падар	[padar]
son	писар	[pisar]
daughter	духтар	[duχtar]
younger daughter	духтари хурдӣ	[duχtari χurdi:]
younger son	писари хурдӣ	[pisari χurdi:]
eldest daughter	духтари калонӣ	[duχtari kaloni:]
eldest son	писари калонӣ	[pisari kaloni:]
brother	бародар	[barodar]
elder brother	ака	[aka]
younger brother	додар	[dodar]
sister	хоҳар	[χohar]
elder sister	апа	[apa]
younger sister	хоҳари хурд	[χohari χurd]
cousin (masc.)	амакписар (ама-, таго-, хола-)	[amakpisar] ([ama], [taʁo], [χola])
cousin (fem.)	амакдухтар (ама-, таго-, хола-)	[amakduχtar] ([ama], [taʁo], [χola])
mom, mommy	модар, оча	[modar], [otʃa]
dad, daddy	дада	[dada]
parents	волидайн	[volidajn]
child	кӯдак	[kœdak]

children	бачагон, кӯдакон	[batʃagon], [kœdakon]
grandmother	модаркалон, онакалон	[modarkalon], [onakalon]
grandfather	бобо	[bobo]
grandson	набера	[nabera]
granddaughter	набера	[nabera]
grandchildren	набераҳо	[naberaho]

uncle	тағо, амак	[taʁo], [amak]
aunt	хола, амма	[χola], [amma]
nephew	ҷиян	[dʒijan]
niece	ҷиян	[dʒijan]

mother-in-law (wife's mother)	модарарӯс	[modararœs]
father-in-law (husband's father)	падаршӯй	[padarʃœj]
son-in-law (daughter's husband)	почо, язна	[potʃo], [jazna]

| stepmother | модарандар | [modarandar] |
| stepfather | падарандар | [padarandar] |

infant	бачаи ширмак	[batʃai ʃirmak]
baby (infant)	кӯдаки ширмак	[kœdaki ʃirmak]
little boy, kid	писарча, кӯдак	[pisartʃa], [kœdak]

| wife | зан | [zan] |
| husband | шавҳар, шӯй | [ʃavhar], [ʃœj] |

| spouse (husband) | завҷ | [zavdʒ] |
| spouse (wife) | завҷа | [zavdʒa] |

married (masc.)	зандор	[zandor]
married (fem.)	шавҳардор	[ʃavhardor]
single (unmarried)	безан	[bezan]
bachelor	безан	[bezan]
divorced (masc.)	ҷудошудагӣ	[dʒudoʃudagi:]

| widow | бева, бевазан | [beva], [bevazan] |
| widower | бева, занмурда | [beva], [zanmurda] |

| relative | хеш | [χeʃ] |
| close relative | хеши наздик | [χeʃi nazdik] |

| distant relative | хеши дур | [χeʃi dur] |
| relatives | хешу табор | [χeʃu tabor] |

orphan (boy)	ятимбача	[jatimbatʃa]
orphan (girl)	ятимдухтар	[jatimduχtar]
guardian (of a minor)	васӣ	[vasi:]
to adopt (a boy)	писар хондан	[pisar χondan]
to adopt (a girl)	духтархонд кардан	[duχtarχond kardan]

60. Friends. Coworkers

friend (masc.)	дӯст, чӯра	[dœst], [ʤœra]
friend (fem.)	дугона	[dugona]
friendship	дӯстӣ, чӯрагӣ	[dœsti:], [ʤœragi:]
to be friends	дӯстӣ кардан	[dœsti: kardan]
buddy (masc.)	дуст, рафик	[dust], [rafik]
buddy (fem.)	шинос	[ʃinos]
partner	шарик	[ʃarik]
chief (boss)	сардор	[sardor]
superior (n)	сардор	[sardor]
owner, proprietor	соҳиб	[sohib]
subordinate (n)	зердаст	[zerdast]
colleague	ҳамкор	[hamkor]
acquaintance (person)	шинос, ошно	[ʃinos], [oʃno]
fellow traveler	ҳамроҳ	[hamroh]
classmate	ҳамсинф	[hamsinf]
neighbor (masc.)	ҳамсоя	[hamsoja]
neighbor (fem.)	ҳамсоязан	[hamsojazan]
neighbors	ҳамсояҳо	[hamsojaho]

HUMAN BODY. MEDICINE

T&P Books Publishing

61. Head

head	сар	[sar]
face	рӯй	[rœj]
nose	бинӣ	[bini:]
mouth	даҳон	[dahon]
eye	чашм, дида	[tʃaʃm], [dida]
eyes	чашмон	[tʃaʃmon]
pupil	гавҳараки чашм	[gavharaki tʃaʃm]
eyebrow	абрӯ, қош	[abrœ], [qoʃ]
eyelash	мижа	[miʒa]
eyelid	пилкҳои чашм	[pilkhoi tʃaʃm]
tongue	забон	[zabon]
tooth	дандон	[dandon]
lips	лабҳо	[labho]
cheekbones	устухони рухсора	[ustuχoni ruχsora]
gum	зираи дандон	[zirai dandon]
palate	ком	[kom]
nostrils	сурохии бинӣ	[suroχi:i bini:]
chin	манаҳ	[manah]
jaw	ҷоғ	[dʒoʁ]
cheek	рухсор	[ruχsor]
forehead	пешона	[peʃona]
temple	чакка	[tʃakka]
ear	гӯш	[gœʃ]
back of the head	пушти сар	[puʃti sar]
neck	гардан	[gardan]
throat	гулӯ	[gulœ]
hair	мӯйи сар	[mœji sar]
hairstyle	ороиши мӯйсар	[oroiʃi mœjsar]
haircut	ороиши мӯйсар	[oroiʃi mœjsar]
wig	мӯи ориятӣ	[mœi orijati:]
mustache	муйлаб, бурут	[mujlab], [burut]
beard	риш	[riʃ]
to have (a beard, etc.)	мондан, доштан	[mondan], [doʃtan]
braid	кокул	[kokul]
sideburns	риши бари рӯй	[riʃi bari rœj]
red-haired (adj)	сурхмуй	[surχmuj]
gray (hair)	сафед	[safed]

| bald (adj) | одамсар | [odamsar] |
| bald patch | тосии сар | [tosi:i sar] |

| ponytail | думча | [dumʧa] |
| bangs | пича | [piʧa] |

62. Human body

| hand | панҷаи даст | [panʤai dast] |
| arm | даст | [dast] |

finger	ангушт	[anguʃt]
toe	чилик, ангушт	[ʧilik], [anguʃt]
thumb	нарангушт	[naranguʃt]
little finger	ангушти хурд	[anguʃti χurd]
nail	нохун	[noχun]

fist	кулак, мушт	[kulak], [muʃt]
palm	каф	[kaf]
wrist	банди даст	[bandi dast]
forearm	бозу	[bozu]
elbow	оринҷ	[orinʤ]
shoulder	китф	[kitʃ]

leg	по	[po]
foot	панҷаи пой	[panʤai poj]
knee	зону	[zonu]
calf (part of leg)	соқи по	[soqi po]
hip	миён	[mijon]
heel	пошна	[poʃna]

body	бадан	[badan]
stomach	шикам	[ʃikam]
chest	сина	[sina]
breast	сина, пистон	[sina], [piston]

flank	паҳлу	[pahlu]
back	пушт	[puʃt]
lower back	камаргоҳ	[kamargoh]
waist	миён	[mijon]

navel (belly button)	ноф	[nof]
buttocks	сурин	[surin]
bottom	сурин	[surin]

beauty mark	хол	[χol]
birthmark (café au lait spot)	хол	[χol]
tattoo	вашм	[vaʃm]
scar	доғи захм	[doʁi zaχm]

63. Diseases

sickness	касалӣ, беморӣ	[kasali:], [bemori:]
to be sick	бемор будан	[bemor budan]
health	тандурустӣ, саломатӣ	[tandurusti:], [salomati:]

runny nose (coryza)	зуком	[zukom]
tonsillitis	дарди гулӯ	[dardi gulœ]
cold (illness)	шамол хӯрдани	[ʃamol χœrdani]
to catch a cold	шамол хӯрдан	[ʃamol χœrdan]

bronchitis	бронхит	[bronχit]
pneumonia	варами шуш	[varami ʃuʃ]
flu, influenza	грипп	[gripp]

nearsighted (adj)	наздикбин	[nazdikbin]
farsighted (adj)	дурбин	[durbin]
strabismus (crossed eyes)	олусӣ	[olusi:]
cross-eyed (adj)	олус	[olus]
cataract	катаракта	[katarakta]
glaucoma	глаукома	[glaukoma]

stroke	сактаи майна	[saktai majna]
heart attack	инфаркт, сактаи дил	[infarkt], [saktai dil]
myocardial infarction	инфаркти миокард	[infarkti miokard]
paralysis	фалач	[faladʒ]
to paralyze (vt)	фалач шудан	[faladʒ ʃudan]

allergy	аллергия	[allergija]
asthma	астма, зиққи нафас	[astma], [ziqqi nafas]
diabetes	диабет	[diabet]

toothache	дарди дандон	[dardi dandon]
caries	кариес	[karies]

diarrhea	шикамрав	[ʃikamrav]
constipation	қабзият	[qabzijat]
stomach upset	вайроншавии меъда	[vajronʃavi:i me'da]
food poisoning	заҳролудшавӣ	[zahroludʃavi:]
to get food poisoning	заҳролуд шудан	[zahrolud ʃudan]

arthritis	артрит	[artrit]
rickets	рахит, чиллаашӯр	[raχit], [tʃillaaʃœr]
rheumatism	тарбод	[tarbod]
atherosclerosis	атеросклероз	[ateroskleroz]

gastritis	гастрит	[gastrit]
appendicitis	варами кӯррӯда	[varami kœrrœda]
cholecystitis	холетсистит	[χoletsistit]
ulcer	захм	[zaχm]
measles	сурхча, сурхак	[surχtʃa], [surχak]

rubella (German measles)	сурхакон	[surχakon]
jaundice	зардча, заъфарма	[zardtʃa], [za'farma]
hepatitis	гепатит, қубод	[gepatit], [qubod]

schizophrenia	маҷзубият	[madʒzubijat]
rabies (hydrophobia)	ҳорӣ	[hori:]
neurosis	невроз, чунун	[nevroz], [tʃunun]
concussion	зарб хӯрдани майна	[zarb χœrdani majna]

cancer	саратон	[saraton]
sclerosis	склероз	[skleroz]
multiple sclerosis	склерози густаришёфта	[sklerozi gustariʃʃofta]

alcoholism	майзадагӣ	[majzadagi:]
alcoholic (n)	майзада	[majzada]
syphilis	оташак	[otaʃak]
AIDS	СПИД	[spid]

tumor	варам	[varam]
malignant (adj)	ганда	[ganda]
benign (adj)	безарар	[bezarar]

fever	табларза, варача	[tablarza], [varadʒa]
malaria	варача	[varadʒa]
gangrene	гангрена	[gangrena]
seasickness	касалии баҳр	[kasali:i bahr]
epilepsy	саръ	[sar']

epidemic	эпидемия	[ɛpidemija]
typhus	арақа, домана	[araqa], [domana]
tuberculosis	сил	[sil]
cholera	вабо	[vabo]
plague (bubonic ~)	тоун	[toun]

64. Symptoms. Treatments. Part 1

symptom	аломат	[alomat]
temperature	ҳарорат, таб	[harorat], [tab]
high temperature (fever)	ҳарорати баланд	[harorati baland]
pulse	набз	[nabz]

dizziness (vertigo)	саргардӣ	[sargardi:]
hot (adj)	гарм	[garm]
shivering	ларза, варача	[larza], [varadʒa]
pale (e.g., ~ face)	рангпарида	[rangparida]

cough	сулфа	[sulfa]
to cough (vi)	сулфидан	[sulfidan]
to sneeze (vi)	атса задан	[atsa zadan]
faint	беҳушӣ	[behuʃi:]

to faint (vi)	бехуш шудан	[behuʃ ʃudan]
bruise (hématome)	доғи кабуд, кабудӣ	[doʁi kabud], [kabudi:]
bump (lump)	ғуррӣ	[ʁurri:]
to bang (bump)	зада шудан	[zada ʃudan]
contusion (bruise)	лат	[lat]
to get a bruise	лату кӯб хӯрдан	[latu kœb χœrdan]

to limp (vi)	лангидан	[langidan]
dislocation	баромадан	[baromadan]
to dislocate (vt)	баровардан	[barovardan]
fracture	шикасти устухон	[ʃikasti ustuχon]
to have a fracture	устухон шикастан	[ustuχon ʃikastan]

cut (e.g., paper ~)	буриш	[buriʃ]
to cut oneself	буридан	[buridan]
bleeding	хунравӣ	[χunravi:]

| burn (injury) | сӯхта | [sœχta] |
| to get burned | сӯзондан | [sœzondan] |

to prick (vt)	халондан	[χalondan]
to prick oneself	халидан	[χalidan]
to injure (vt)	осеб дидан	[oseb didan]
injury	захм	[zaχm]
wound	захм, реш	[zaχm], [reʃ]
trauma	захм	[zaχm]

to be delirious	алой гуфтан	[aloi: guftan]
to stutter (vi)	тутила шудан	[tutila ʃudan]
sunstroke	офтобзанӣ	[oftobzani:]

65. Symptoms. Treatments. Part 2

| pain, ache | дард | [dard] |
| splinter (in foot, etc.) | хор, зиреба | [χor], [zireba] |

sweat (perspiration)	арақ	[araq]
to sweat (perspire)	арақ кардан	[araq kardan]
vomiting	қайкунӣ	[qajkuni:]
convulsions	рагкашӣ	[ragkaʃi:]

pregnant (adj)	ҳомила	[homila]
to be born	таваллуд шудан	[tavallud ʃudan]
delivery, labor	зоиш	[zoiʃ]
to deliver (~ a baby)	зоидан	[zoidan]
abortion	аборт, бачапартой	[abort], [batʃapartoi:]

in-breath (inhalation)	нафасгирӣ	[nafasgiri:]
out-breath (exhalation)	нафасбарорӣ	[nafasbarori:]
to exhale (breathe out)	нафас баровардаи	[nafas barovardai]

to inhale (vi)	нафас кашидан	[nafas kaʃidan]
disabled person	инвалид	[invalid]
cripple	маъюб	[ma'jub]
drug addict	нашъаманд	[naʃ'amand]

deaf (adj)	кар, гӯшкар	[kar], [gœʃkar]
mute (adj)	гунг	[gung]
deaf mute (adj)	кару гунг	[karu gung]

mad, insane (adj)	девона	[devona]
madman (demented person)	девона	[devona]
madwoman	девона	[devona]
to go insane	аз ақл бегона шудан	[az aql begona ʃudan]

gene	ген	[gen]
immunity	сироятнопазирӣ	[sirojatnopaziri:]
hereditary (adj)	меросӣ, ирсӣ	[merosi:], [irsi:]
congenital (adj)	модарзод	[modarzod]

virus	вирус	[virus]
microbe	микроб	[mikrob]
bacterium	бактерия	[bakterija]
infection	сироят	[sirojat]

66. Symptoms. Treatments. Part 3

hospital	касалхона	[kasalχona]
patient	бемор	[bemor]

diagnosis	ташхиси касалӣ	[taʃχisi kasali:]
cure	муолича	[muolidʒa]
medical treatment	табобат	[tabobat]
to get treatment	табобат гирифтан	[tabobat giriftan]
to treat (~ a patient)	табобат кардан	[tabobat kardan]
to nurse (look after)	нигоҳубин кардан	[nigohubin kardan]
care (nursing ~)	нигоҳубин	[nigohubin]

operation, surgery	чарроҳи	[dʒarrohi]
to bandage (head, limb)	бо бандина бастан	[bo bandina bastan]
bandaging	чароҳатбандӣ	[dʒarohatbandi:]

vaccination	доругузаронӣ	[doruguzaroni:]
to vaccinate (vt)	эмгузаронӣ кардан	[ɛmguzaroni: kardan]
injection, shot	сӯзанзанӣ	[sœzanzani:]
to give an injection	сӯзандору кардан	[sœzandoru kardan]

attack	хуруч	[χurudʒ]
amputation	ампутатсия	[amputatsija]
to amputate (vt)	ампутатсия кардан	[amputatsija kardan]

coma	кома, игмо	[koma], [igmo]
to be in a coma	дар кома будан	[dar koma budan]
intensive care	шӯъбаи эхё	[ʃœ'bai ɛhjɔ]

to recover (~ from flu)	сихат шудан	[sihat ʃudan]
condition (patient's ~)	ахвол	[ahvol]
consciousness	хуш	[huʃ]
memory (faculty)	хофиза	[hofiza]

to pull out (tooth)	кандан	[kandan]
filling	пломба	[plomba]
to fill (a tooth)	пломба занондан	[plomba zanondan]

| hypnosis | гипноз | [gipnoz] |
| to hypnotize (vt) | гипноз кардан | [gipnoz kardan] |

67. Medicine. Drugs. Accessories

medicine, drug	дору	[doru]
remedy	дору	[doru]
to prescribe (vt)	таъйин кардан	[ta'jin kardan]
prescription	нусхаи даво	[nusχai davo]

tablet, pill	хаб	[hab]
ointment	мархам	[marham]
ampule	ампул	[ampul]
mixture	доруи обакӣ	[dorui obaki:]
syrup	сироп	[sirop]
pill	хаб	[hab]
powder	хока	[χoka]

gauze bandage	дока	[doka]
cotton wool	пахта	[paχta]
iodine	йод	[jod]

Band-Aid	лейкопластир	[lejkoplastir]
eyedropper	қатрачакон	[qatratʃakon]
thermometer	хароратсанч	[haroratsandʒ]
syringe	обдуздак	[obduzdak]

| wheelchair | аробачаи маъюбӣ | [arobatʃai ma'jubi:] |
| crutches | бағаласо | [baʁalaso] |

painkiller	доруи дард	[dorui dard]
laxative	мусхил	[mushil]
spirits (ethanol)	спирт	[spirt]
medicinal herbs	растанихои доругӣ	[rastanihoi dorugi:]
herbal (~ tea)	… и алаф	[i alaf]

APARTMENT

T&P Books Publishing

68. Apartment

apartment	манзил	[manzil]
room	хона, ӯтоқ	[χona], [œtoq]
bedroom	хонаи хоб	[χonai χob]
dining room	хонаи хӯрокхӯрӣ	[χonai χœrokχœri:]
living room	меҳмонхона	[mehmonχona]
study (home office)	утоқ	[utoq]
entry room	мадхал, даҳлез	[madχal], [dahlez]
bathroom (room with a bath or shower)	ваннахона	[vannaχona]
half bath	ҳоҷатхона	[hodʒatχona]
ceiling	шифт	[ʃift]
floor	фарш	[farʃ]
corner	кунҷ	[kundʒ]

69. Furniture. Interior

furniture	мебел	[mebel]
table	миз	[miz]
chair	курсӣ	[kursi:]
bed	кат	[kat]
couch, sofa	диван	[divan]
armchair	курсӣ	[kursi:]
bookcase	чевони китобмонӣ	[dʒevoni kitobmoni:]
shelf	раф, рафча	[raf], [raftʃa]
wardrobe	чевони либос	[dʒevoni libos]
coat rack (wall-mounted ~)	либосовезак	[libosovezak]
coat stand	либосовезак	[libosovezak]
bureau, dresser	чевон	[dʒevon]
coffee table	мизи қаҳва	[mizi qahva]
mirror	оина	[oina]
carpet	гилем, қолин	[gilem], [qolin]
rug, small carpet	гилемча	[gilemtʃa]
fireplace	оташдон	[otaʃdon]
candle	шамъ	[ʃam']
candlestick	шамъдон	[ʃam'don]

drapes	парда	[parda]
wallpaper	зардеворй	[zardevori:]
blinds (jalousie)	жалюзи	[ʒaljuzi]

table lamp	чароғи мизй	[ʧaroʁi mizi:]
wall lamp (sconce)	чароғак	[ʧaroʁak]
floor lamp	торшер	[torʃer]
chandelier	қандил	[qandil]

leg (of chair, table)	поя	[poja]
armrest	оринчмонаки курсй	[orinʤmonaki kursi:]
back (backrest)	пуштаки курсй	[puʃtaki kursi:]
drawer	ғаладон	[ʁaladon]

70. Bedding

bedclothes	чилдхои болишту бистар	[ʤildhoi boliʃtu bistar]
pillow	болишт	[boliʃt]
pillowcase	чилди болишт	[ʤildi boliʃt]
duvet, comforter	кӯрпа	[kœrpa]
sheet	чойпӯш	[ʤojpœʃ]
bedspread	болопӯш	[bolopœʃ]

71. Kitchen

kitchen	ошхона	[oʃχona]
gas	газ	[gaz]
gas stove (range)	плитаи газ	[plitai gaz]
electric stove	плитаи электрикй	[plitai ɛlektriki:]
microwave oven	микроволновка	[mikrovolnovka]

refrigerator	яхдон	[jaχdon]
freezer	яхдон	[jaχdon]
dishwasher	мошини зарфшӯй	[moʃini zarfʃœj]

meat grinder	мошини гӯштқӯбй	[moʃini gœʃtkœbi:]
juicer	шарбатафшурак	[ʃarbatafʃurak]
toaster	тостер	[toster]
mixer	миксер	[mikser]

coffee machine	қаҳвачӯшонак	[qahvaʤœʃonak]
coffee pot	зарфи қаҳвачӯшонй	[zarfi qahvaʤœʃoni:]
coffee grinder	дастоси қаҳва	[dastosi qahva]

kettle	чойник	[ʧojnik]
teapot	чойник	[ʧojnik]
lid	сарпӯш	[sarpœʃ]

tea strainer	ғалберча	[ʁalbertʃa]
spoon	қошуқ	[qoʃuq]
teaspoon	чойкошук	[tʃojkoʃuk]
soup spoon	қошуқи ошхӯрӣ	[qoʃuqi oʃχœri:]
fork	чангча, чангол	[tʃangtʃa], [tʃangol]
knife	корд	[kord]

tableware (dishes)	табақ	[tabaq]
plate (dinner ~)	тақсимча	[taqsimtʃa]
saucer	тақсимӣ, тақсимича	[taqsimi:], [taqsimitʃa]

shot glass	рюмка	[rjumka]
glass (tumbler)	стакан	[stakan]
cup	косача	[kosatʃa]

sugar bowl	шакардон	[ʃakardon]
salt shaker	намакдон	[namakdon]
pepper shaker	қаламфурдон	[qalamfurdon]
butter dish	равғандон	[ravʁandon]

stock pot (soup pot)	дегча	[degtʃa]
frying pan (skillet)	тоба	[toba]
ladle	кафлез, обгардон, сархумӣ	[kaflez], [obgardon], [sarχumi:]
tray (serving ~)	лаълӣ	[la'li:]

bottle	шиша, суроҳӣ	[ʃiʃa], [surohi:]
jar (glass)	банкаи шишагӣ	[bankai ʃiʃagi:]
can	банкаи тунукагӣ	[bankai tunukagi:]

bottle opener	саркушояк	[sarkuʃojak]
can opener	саркушояк	[sarkuʃojak]
corkscrew	пӯккашак	[pœkkaʃak]
filter	филтр	[filtr]
to filter (vt)	полоидан	[poloidan]

trash, garbage (food waste, etc.)	ахлот	[aχlot]
trash can (kitchen ~)	сатили ахлот	[satili aχlot]

72. Bathroom

bathroom	ваннахона	[vannaχona]
water	об	[ob]
faucet	чуммак, мил	[dʒummak], [mil]
hot water	оби гарм	[obi garm]
cold water	оби сард	[obi sard]

toothpaste	хамираи дандон	[χamirai dandon]
to brush one's teeth	дандон шустан	[dandon ʃustan]

toothbrush	чӯткаи дандоншӯй	[tʃœtkai dandonʃœi:]
to shave (vi)	риш гирифтан	[riʃ giriftan]
shaving foam	кафки ришгирй	[kafki riʃgiri:]
razor	ришгирак	[riʃgirak]

to wash (one's hands, etc.)	шустан	[ʃustan]
to take a bath	шустушӯ кардан	[ʃustuʃœ kardan]
to take a shower	ба душ даромадан	[ba duʃ daromadan]

bathtub	ванна	[vanna]
toilet (toilet bowl)	нишастгоҳи халоҷо	[niʃastgohi xalodʒo]
sink (washbasin)	дастшӯяк	[dastʃœjak]

| soap | собун | [sobun] |
| soap dish | собундон | [sobundon] |

sponge	исфанҷ	[isfandʒ]
shampoo	шампун	[ʃampun]
towel	сачоқ	[satʃoq]
bathrobe	халат	[xalat]

laundry (process)	ҷомашӯй	[dʒomaʃœi:]
washing machine	мошини ҷомашӯй	[moʃini dʒomaʃœi:]
to do the laundry	ҷомашӯй кардан	[dʒomaʃœi: kardan]
laundry detergent	хокаи ҷомашӯй	[xokai dʒomaʃœi:]

73. Household appliances

TV set	телевизор	[televizor]
tape recorder	магнитафон	[magnitafon]
VCR (video recorder)	видеомагнитафон	[videomagnitafon]
radio	радио	[radio]
player (CD, MP3, etc.)	плеер	[pleer]

video projector	видеопроектор	[videoproektor]
home movie theater	кинотеатри хонагй	[kinoteatri xonagi:]
DVD player	DVD-монак	[εœε-monak]
amplifier	қувватафзо	[quvvatafzo]
video game console	плейстейшн	[plejstejʃn]

video camera	видеокамера	[videokamera]
camera (photo)	фотоаппарат	[fotoapparat]
digital camera	суратгираки рақамй	[suratgiraki raqami:]

vacuum cleaner	чангкашак	[tʃangkaʃak]
iron (e.g., steam ~)	дарзмол	[darzmol]
ironing board	тахтаи дарзмолкунй	[taxtai darzmolkuni:]

| telephone | телефон | [telefon] |
| cell phone | телефони мобилй | [telefoni mobili:] |

typewriter	**мошинаи хатнависӣ**	[moʃinai χatnavisi:]
sewing machine	**мошинаи чокдӯзӣ**	[moʃinai ʧokdœzi:]
microphone	**микрофон**	[mikrofon]
headphones	**гӯшак, гӯшпӯшак**	[gœʃak], [gœʃpœʃak]
remote control (TV)	**пулт**	[pult]
CD, compact disc	**компакт-диск**	[kompakt-disk]
cassette, tape	**кассета**	[kasseta]
vinyl record	**пластинка**	[plastinka]

THE EARTH. WEATHER

T&P Books Publishing

74. Outer space

space	кайҳон	[kajhon]
space (as adj)	... и кайҳон	[i kajhon]
outer space	фазои кайҳон	[fazoi kajhon]
world	чаҳон	[dʒahon]
universe	коинот	[koinot]
galaxy	галактика	[galaktika]
star	ситора	[sitora]
constellation	бурҷ	[burdʒ]
planet	сайёра	[sajjora]
satellite	радиф	[radif]
meteorite	метеорит, шиҳобпора	[meteorit], [ʃihobpora]
comet	ситораи думдор	[sitorai dumdor]
asteroid	астероид	[asteroid]
orbit	мадор	[mador]
to revolve	давр задан	[davr zadan]
(~ around the Earth)		
atmosphere	атмосфера	[atmosfera]
the Sun	Офтоб	[oftob]
solar system	манзумаи шамсӣ	[manzumai ʃamsi:]
solar eclipse	гирифтани офтоб	[giriftani oftob]
the Earth	Замин	[zamin]
the Moon	Моҳ	[moh]
Mars	Миррих	[mirriχ]
Venus	Зӯҳра, Ноҳид	[zœhra], [nohid]
Jupiter	Муштарӣ	[muʃtari:]
Saturn	Кайвон	[kajvon]
Mercury	Уторид	[utorid]
Uranus	Уран	[uran]
Neptune	Нептун	[neptun]
Pluto	Плутон	[pluton]
Milky Way	Роҳи Каҳкашон	[rohi kahkaʃon]
Great Bear (Ursa Major)	Дубби Акбар	[dubbi akbar]
North Star	Ситораи қутбӣ	[sitorai qutbi:]
Martian	миррихӣ	[mirriχi:]
extraterrestrial (n)	инопланетянҳо	[inoplanetjanho]

| alien | махлуқи кайҳонӣ | [maχluqi: kajhoni:] |
| flying saucer | табақи парвозкунанда | [tabaqi parvozkunanda] |

spaceship	киштии кайҳонӣ	[kiʃti:i kajhoni:]
space station	стантсияи мадорӣ	[stantsijai madori:]
blast-off	оғоз	[oʁoz]

engine	муҳаррик	[muharrik]
nozzle	сопло	[soplo]
fuel	сӯзишворӣ	[sœziʃvori:]

cockpit, flight deck	кабина	[kabina]
antenna	антенна	[antenna]
porthole	иллюминатор	[illjuminator]
solar panel	батареи офтобӣ	[batarei oftobi:]
spacesuit	скафандр	[skafandr]

| weightlessness | бевазнӣ | [bevazni:] |
| oxygen | оксиген | [oksigen] |

| docking (in space) | пайваст | [pajvast] |
| to dock (vi, vt) | пайваст кардан | [pajvast kardan] |

observatory	расадхона	[rasadχona]
telescope	телескоп	[teleskop]
to observe (vt)	мушоҳида кардан	[muʃohida kardan]
to explore (vt)	таҳқиқ кардан	[tahqiq kardan]

75. The Earth

the Earth	Замин	[zamin]
the globe (the Earth)	кураи замин	[kurai zamin]
planet	сайёра	[sajjɔra]

atmosphere	атмосфера	[atmosfera]
geography	география	[geografija]
nature	табиат	[tabiat]
globe (table ~)	глобус	[globus]
map	харита	[χarita]
atlas	атлас	[atlas]

Asia	Осиё	[osijɔ]
Africa	Африқо	[afriqo]
Australia	Австралия	[avstralija]

America	Америка	[amerika]
North America	Америкаи Шимолӣ	[amerikai ʃimoli:]
South America	Америкаи Ҷанубӣ	[amerikai ʤanubi:]
Antarctica	Антарктида	[antarktida]
the Arctic	Арктика	[arktika]

76. Cardinal directions

north	шимол	[ʃimol]
to the north	ба шимол	[ba ʃimol]
in the north	дар шимол	[dar ʃimol]
northern (adj)	шимолӣ, ... и шимол	[ʃimoli:], [i ʃimol]

south	ҷануб	[ʤanub]
to the south	ба ҷануб	[ba ʤanub]
in the south	дар ҷануб	[dar ʤanub]
southern (adj)	ҷанубӣ, ... и ҷануб	[ʤanubi:], [i ʤanub]

west	ғарб	[ʁarb]
to the west	ба ғарб	[ba ʁarb]
in the west	дар ғарб	[dar ʁarb]
western (adj)	ғарбӣ, ... и ғарб	[ʁarbi:], [i ʁarb]

east	шарқ	[ʃarq]
to the east	ба шарқ	[ba ʃarq]
in the east	дар шарқ	[dar ʃarq]
eastern (adj)	шарқӣ	[ʃarqi:]

77. Sea. Ocean

sea	баҳр	[bahr]
ocean	уқёнус	[uqjɔnus]
gulf (bay)	халиҷ	[χaliʤ]
straits	гулӯгоҳ	[gulœgoh]

land (solid ground)	хушкӣ, замин	[χuʃki:], [zamin]
continent (mainland)	материк, қитъа	[materik], [qit'a]

island	ҷазира	[ʤazira]
peninsula	нимҷазира	[nimʤazira]
archipelago	галаҷазира	[galaʤazira]

bay, cove	халиҷ	[χaliʤ]
harbor	бандар	[bandar]
lagoon	лагуна	[laguna]
cape	димоға	[dimoʁa]

atoll	атолл	[atoll]
reef	харсанги зериобӣ	[χarsangi zeriobi:]
coral	марҷон	[marʤon]
coral reef	обсанги марҷонӣ	[obsangi marʤoni:]

deep (adj)	чуқур	[ʧuqur]
depth (deep water)	чуқурӣ	[ʧuquri:]
abyss	қаър	[qa'r]

trench (e.g., Mariana ~)	чуқурй	[tʃuquri:]
current (Ocean ~)	ҷараён	[dʒarajɔn]
to surround (bathe)	шустан	[ʃustan]
shore	соҳил, соҳили баҳр	[sohil], [sohili bahr]
coast	соҳил	[sohil]
flow (flood tide)	мадд	[madd]
ebb (ebb tide)	ҷазр	[dʒazr]
shoal	пастоб	[pastob]
bottom (~ of the sea)	қаър	[qa'r]
wave	мавҷ	[mavdʒ]
crest (~ of a wave)	теғаи мавҷ	[teʁai mavdʒ]
spume (sea foam)	кафк	[kafk]
storm (sea storm)	тӯфон, бӯрои	[tœfon], [bœroi]
hurricane	тундбод	[tundbod]
tsunami	сунами	[sunami]
calm (dead ~)	сукунати ҳаво	[sukunati havo]
quiet, calm (adj)	ором	[orom]
pole	қутб	[qutb]
polar (adj)	қутбӣ	[qutbi:]
latitude	арз	[arz]
longitude	тӯл	[tœl]
parallel	параллел	[parallel]
equator	хати истиво	[χati istivo]
sky	осмон	[osmon]
horizon	уфуқ	[ufuq]
air	ҳаво	[havo]
lighthouse	мино	[mino]
to dive (vi)	ғӯта задан	[ʁœta zadan]
to sink (ab. boat)	ғарқ шудан	[ʁarq ʃudan]
treasures	ганҷ	[gandʒ]

78. Seas' and Oceans' names

Atlantic Ocean	Уқёнуси Атлантик	[uqjɔnusi atlantik]
Indian Ocean	Уқёнуси Ҳинд	[uqjɔnusi hind]
Pacific Ocean	Уқёнуси Ором	[uqjɔnusi orom]
Arctic Ocean	Уқёнуси яхбастаи шимолӣ	[uqjɔnusi jaχbastai ʃimoli:]
Black Sea	Баҳри Сиёҳ	[bahri sijɔh]
Red Sea	Баҳри Сурх	[bahri surχ]
Yellow Sea	Баҳри Зард	[bahri zard]

White Sea	Баҳри Сафед	[bahri safed]
Caspian Sea	Баҳри Хазар	[bahri χazar]
Dead Sea	Баҳри Майит	[bahri majit]
Mediterranean Sea	Баҳри Миёназамин	[bahri mijɔnazamin]

| Aegean Sea | Баҳри Эгей | [bahri ɛgej] |
| Adriatic Sea | Баҳри Адриатика | [bahri adriatika] |

Arabian Sea	Баҳри Арави	[bahri aravi]
Sea of Japan	Баҳри Ҷопон	[bahri ʤɔpon]
Bering Sea	Баҳри Беринг	[bahri bering]
South China Sea	Баҳри Хитойи Ҷанубй	[bahri χitoji ʤanubi:]

Coral Sea	Баҳри Марҷон	[bahri marʤon]
Tasman Sea	Баҳри Тасман	[bahri tasman]
Caribbean Sea	Баҳри Кариб	[bahri karib]

| Barents Sea | Баҳри Баренс | [bahri barens] |
| Kara Sea | Баҳри Кара | [bahri kara] |

North Sea	Баҳри Шимолй	[bahri ʃimoli:]
Baltic Sea	Баҳри Балтика	[bahri baltika]
Norwegian Sea	Баҳри Норвегия	[bahri norvegija]

79. Mountains

mountain	кӯҳ	[kœh]
mountain range	силсилакӯҳ	[silsilakœh]
mountain ridge	қаторкӯҳ	[qatorkœh]

summit, top	кулла	[kulla]
peak	қулла	[qulla]
foot (~ of the mountain)	доманаи кӯҳ	[domanai kœh]
slope (mountainside)	нишебй	[niʃebi:]

volcano	вулқон	[vulqon]
active volcano	вулқони амалкунанда	[vulqoni amalkunanda]
dormant volcano	вулқони хомӯшшуда	[vulqoni χomœʃʃuda]

eruption	оташфишонй	[otaʃfiʃoni:]
crater	танӯра	[tanœra]
magma	магма, тафта	[magma], [tafta]
lava	гудоза	[gudoza]
molten (~ lava)	тафта	[tafta]

canyon	оббурда, дара	[obburda], [dara]
gorge	дара	[dara]
crevice	тангно	[tangno]
abyss (chasm)	партгоҳ	[partgoh]

pass, col	агба	[aʁba]
plateau	пуштаи кӯҳ	[puʃtai kœh]
cliff	шух	[ʃux]
hill	теппа	[teppa]

glacier	пирях	[pirjaχ]
waterfall	шаршара	[ʃarʃara]
geyser	гейзер	[gejzer]
lake	кул	[kul]

plain	ҳамворӣ	[hamvoriː]
landscape	манзара	[manzara]
echo	акси садо	[aksi sado]

alpinist	кӯҳнавард	[kœhnavard]
rock climber	шухпаймо	[ʃuxpajmo]
to conquer (in climbing)	фатҳ кардан	[fath kardan]
climb (an easy ~)	болобарой	[bolobaroiː]

80. Mountains names

The Alps	Кӯҳҳои Алп	[kœhhoi alp]
Mont Blanc	Монблан	[monblan]
The Pyrenees	Кӯҳҳои Пиреней	[kœhhoi pirenej]

The Carpathians	Кӯҳҳои Карпат	[kœhhoi karpat]
The Ural Mountains	Кӯҳҳои Урал	[kœhhoi ural]
The Caucasus Mountains	Кӯҳҳои Кавказ	[kœhhoi kavkaz]
Mount Elbrus	Елбруз	[elbruz]

The Altai Mountains	Алтай	[altaj]
The Tian Shan	Тиёншон	[tijɔnʃon]
The Pamir Mountains	Кӯҳҳои Помир	[kœhhoi pomir]
The Himalayas	Ҳимолой	[himoloj]
Mount Everest	Эверест	[ɛverest]

| The Andes | Кӯҳҳои Анд | [kœhhoi and] |
| Mount Kilimanjaro | Килиманҷаро | [kilimanʤaro] |

81. Rivers

river	дарё	[darjɔ]
spring (natural source)	чашма	[tʃaʃma]
riverbed (river channel)	маҷрои дарё	[madʒroi darjɔ]
basin (river valley)	ҳавза	[havza]
to flow into ...	рехтан ба ...	[reχtan ba]
tributary	шохоб	[ʃoχob]
bank (of river)	соҳил	[sohil]

current (stream)	чараён	[dʒarajɔn]
downstream (adv)	мувофиқи рафти об	[muvofiqi rafti ob]
upstream (adv)	муқобили самти об	[muqobili samti ob]
inundation	обхезй	[obχezi:]
flooding	обхез	[obχez]
to overflow (vi)	дамидан	[damidan]
to flood (vt)	зер кардан	[zer kardan]
shallow (shoal)	тунукоба	[tunukoba]
rapids	мавчрез	[mavdʒrez]
dam	сарбанд	[sarband]
canal	канал	[kanal]
reservoir (artificial lake)	обанбор	[obanbor]
sluice, lock	шлюз	[ʃljuz]
water body (pond, etc.)	обанбор	[obanbor]
swamp (marshland)	ботлоқ, ботқоқ	[botloq], [botqoq]
bog, marsh	ботлоқ	[botloq]
whirlpool	гирдоб	[girdob]
stream (brook)	чӯй	[dʒœj]
drinking (ab. water)	нӯшиданй	[nœʃidani:]
fresh (~ water)	ширин	[ʃirin]
ice	ях	[jaχ]
to freeze over (ab. river, etc.)	ях бастан	[jaχ bastan]

82. Rivers' names

Seine	Сена	[sena]
Loire	Луара	[luara]
Thames	Темза	[temza]
Rhine	Рейн	[rejn]
Danube	Дунай	[dunaj]
Volga	Волга	[volga]
Don	Дон	[don]
Lena	Лена	[lena]
Yellow River	Хуанхе	[χuanχe]
Yangtze	Янсзи	[janszi]
Mekong	Меконг	[mekong]
Ganges	Ганга	[ganga]
Nile River	Нил	[nil]
Congo River	Конго	[kongo]

Okavango River	Окаванго	[okavango]
Zambezi River	Замбези	[zambezi]
Limpopo River	Лимпопо	[limpopo]
Mississippi River	Миссисипи	[missisipi]

83. Forest

| forest, wood | чангал | [dʒangal] |
| forest (as adj) | чангалй | [dʒangali:] |

thick forest	чангалзор	[dʒangalzor]
grove	дарахтзор	[daraχtzor]
forest clearing	чаман	[tʃaman]

| thicket | буттазор | [buttazor] |
| scrubland | буттазор | [buttazor] |

| footpath (troddenpath) | пайраха | [pajraha] |
| gully | оббурда | [obburda] |

tree	дарахт	[daraχt]
leaf	барг	[barg]
leaves (foliage)	баргхои дарахт	[barghoi daraχt]

fall of leaves	баргрезй	[bargrezi:]
to fall (ab. leaves)	рехтан	[reχtan]
top (of the tree)	нӯг	[nœg]

branch	шох, шохча	[ʃoχ], [ʃoχtʃa]
bough	шохи дарахг	[ʃoχi daraχg]
bud (on shrub, tree)	муғча	[muʁdʒa]
needle (of pine tree)	сӯзан	[sœzan]
pine cone	чалгӯза	[dʒalʁœza]

hollow (in a tree)	сӯрохи дарахт	[sœroχi daraχt]
nest	ошёна, лона	[oʃjona], [lona]
burrow (animal hole)	хона	[χona]

trunk	тана	[tana]
root	реша	[reʃa]
bark	пӯсти дарахт	[pœsti daraχt]
moss	ушна	[uʃna]

to uproot (remove trees or tree stumps)	реша кофтан	[reʃa koftan]
to chop down	зада буридан	[zada buridan]
to deforest (vt)	бурида нест кардан	[burida nest kardan]
tree stump	кундаи дарахт	[kundai daraχt]
campfire	гулхан	[gulχan]
forest fire	сӯхтор, оташ	[sœχtor], [otaʃ]

to extinguish (vt)	хомӯш кардан	[χomœʃ kardan]
forest ranger	ҷангалбон	[dʒangalbon]
protection	нигоҳбонӣ	[nigohboni:]
to protect (~ nature)	нигоҳбонӣ кардан	[nigohboni: kardan]
poacher	кӯруқшикан	[qœruqʃikan]
steel trap	қапқон, дом	[qapqon], [dom]

| to gather, to pick (vt) | чидан | [tʃidan] |
| to lose one's way | роҳ гум кардан | [roh gum kardan] |

84. Natural resources

natural resources	захираҳои табий	[zaχirahoi tabi:i:]
minerals	маъданҳои фоиданок	[ma'danhoi foidanok]
deposits	кон, маъдаи	[kon], [ma'dai]
field (e.g., oilfield)	кон	[kon]

to mine (extract)	кандан	[kandan]
mining (extraction)	канданӣ	[kandani:]
ore	маъдан	[ma'dan]
mine (e.g., for coal)	кон	[kon]
shaft (mine ~)	чоҳ	[tʃoh]
miner	конкан	[konkan]

| gas (natural ~) | газ | [gaz] |
| gas pipeline | қубури газ | [quburi gaz] |

oil (petroleum)	нефт	[neft]
oil pipeline	қубури нефт	[quburi neft]
oil well	чоҳи нафт	[tʃohi naft]
derrick (tower)	бурҷи нафткашӣ	[burdʒi naftkaʃi:]
tanker	танкер	[tanker]

sand	рег	[reg]
limestone	оҳаксанг	[ohaksang]
gravel	сангреза, шағал	[sangreza], [ʃaʁal]
peat	торф	[torf]
clay	гил	[gil]
coal	ангишт	[angiʃt]

iron (ore)	оҳан	[ohan]
gold	зар, тилло	[zar], [tillo]
silver	нуқра	[nuqra]
nickel	никел	[nikel]
copper	мис	[mis]

zinc	руҳ	[ruh]
manganese	манган	[mangan]
mercury	симоб	[simob]
lead	сурб	[surb]

mineral	минерал, маъдан	[mineral], [ma'dan]
crystal	булӯр, шӯша	[bulœr], [ʃœʃa]
marble	мармар	[marmar]
uranium	уран	[uran]

85. Weather

weather	обу ҳаво	[obu havo]
weather forecast	пешгӯии ҳаво	[peʃɡœi:i havo]
temperature	ҳарорат	[harorat]
thermometer	ҳароратсанҷ	[haroratsandʒ]
barometer	барометр, ҳавосанҷ	[barometr], [havosandʒ]

| humid (adj) | намнок | [namnok] |
| humidity | намй, рутубат | [nami:], [rutubat] |

heat (extreme ~)	гармй	[garmi:]
hot (torrid)	тафсон	[tafson]
it's hot	ҳаво тафсон аст	[havo tafson ast]

| it's warm | ҳаво гарм аст | [havo garm ast] |
| warm (moderately hot) | гарм | [garm] |

| it's cold | ҳаво сард аст | [havo sard ast] |
| cold (adj) | хунук, сард | [χunuk], [sard] |

sun	офтоб	[oftob]
to shine (vi)	тобидан	[tobidan]
sunny (day)	... и офтоб	[i oftob]
to come up (vi)	баромадан	[baromadan]
to set (vi)	паст шудан	[past ʃudan]

cloud	абр	[abr]
cloudy (adj)	... и абр, абрй	[i abr], [abri:]
rain cloud	абри сиёҳ	[abri sijɔh]
somber (gloomy)	абрнок	[abrnok]

rain	борон	[boron]
it's raining	борон меборад	[boron meborad]
rainy (~ day, weather)	серборон	[serboron]
to drizzle (vi)	сим-сим боридан	[sim-sim boridan]

pouring rain	борони сахт	[boroni saχt]
downpour	борони сел	[boroni sel]
heavy (e.g., ~ rain)	сахт	[saχt]
puddle	кӯлмак	[kœlmak]
to get wet (in rain)	шилтиқ шудан	[ʃiltiq ʃudan]

| fog (mist) | туман | [tuman] |
| foggy | ... и туман | [i tuman] |

| snow | барф | [barf] |
| it's snowing | барф меборад | [barf meborad] |

86. Severe weather. Natural disasters

thunderstorm	раъду барк	[ra'du bark]
lightning (~ strike)	барқ	[barq]
to flash (vi)	дурахшидан	[duraxʃidan]

thunder	тундар	[tundar]
to thunder (vi)	гулдуррос задан	[guldurros zadan]
it's thundering	раъд гулдуррос мезанад	[ra'd guldurros mezanad]

| hail | жола | [ʒola] |
| it's hailing | жола меборад | [ʒola meborad] |

| to flood (vt) | зер кардан | [zer kardan] |
| flood, inundation | обхезй | [obχezi:] |

earthquake	заминчунбй	[zamindʒunbi:]
tremor, quake	заминчунбй,такон	[zamindʒunbi:,takon]
epicenter	эпимарказ	[ɛpimarkaz]

| eruption | оташфишонй | [otaʃfiʃoni:] |
| lava | гудоза | [gudoza] |

twister	гирдбод	[girdbod]
tornado	торнадо	[tornado]
typhoon	тӯфон	[tœfon]

hurricane	тундбод	[tundbod]
storm	тӯфон, бӯрои	[tœfon], [bœroi]
tsunami	сунами	[sunami]

cyclone	сиклон	[siklon]
bad weather	ҳавои бад	[havoi bad]
fire (accident)	сӯхтор, оташ	[sœχtor], [otaʃ]
disaster	садама, фалокат	[sadama], [falokat]
meteorite	метеорит, шиҳобпора	[meteorit], [ʃihobpora]

avalanche	тарма	[tarma]
snowslide	тарма	[tarma]
blizzard	бӯрони барфй	[bœroni barfi:]
snowstorm	бӯрон	[bœron]

FAUNA

T&P Books Publishing

87. Mammals. Predators

predator	дарранда	[darranda]
tiger	бабр, паланг	[babr], [palang]
lion	шер	[ʃer]
wolf	гург	[gurg]
fox	рӯбоҳ	[rœboh]
jaguar	юзи ало	[juzi alo]
leopard	паланг	[palang]
cheetah	юз	[juz]
black panther	пантера	[pantera]
puma	пума	[puma]
snow leopard	шерпаланг	[ʃerpalang]
lynx	силовсин	[silovsin]
coyote	койот	[kojɔt]
jackal	шагол	[ʃagol]
hyena	кафтор	[kaftor]

88. Wild animals

animal	ҳайвон	[hajvon]
beast (animal)	ҳайвони ваҳшӣ	[hajvoni vahʃi:]
squirrel	санҷоб	[sandʒob]
hedgehog	хорпушт	[χorpuʃt]
hare	заргӯш	[zargœʃ]
rabbit	харгӯш	[χargœʃ]
badger	қашқалдоқ	[qaʃqaldoq]
raccoon	енот	[enot]
hamster	миримӯшон	[mirimœʃon]
marmot	суғур	[suʁur]
mole	кӯрмуш	[kœrmuʃ]
mouse	муш	[muʃ]
rat	калламуш	[kallamuʃ]
bat	кӯршапарак	[kœrʃaparak]
ermine	қоқум	[qoqum]
sable	самур	[samur]
marten	савсор	[savsor]

| weasel | росу | [rosu] |
| mink | вашақ | [vaʃaq] |

| beaver | кундуз | [kunduz] |
| otter | сагоби | [sagobi] |

horse	асп	[asp]
moose	шоҳгавазн	[ʃohgavazn]
deer	гавазн	[gavazn]
camel	шутур, уштур	[ʃutur], [uʃtur]

bison	бизон	[bizon]
aurochs	гови ваҳшӣ	[govi vahʃiː]
buffalo	говмеш	[govmeʃ]

zebra	гӯрхар	[gœrxar]
antelope	антилопа, ғизол	[antilopa], [ʁizol]
roe deer	оху	[ohu]
fallow deer	оху	[ohu]
chamois	нахчир, бузи кӯҳӣ	[naxtʃir], [buzi kœhiː]
wild boar	хуки ваҳши	[xuki vahʃi]

whale	кит, наҳанг	[kit], [nahang]
seal	тюлен	[tjulen]
walrus	морж	[morʒ]
fur seal	гурбаи обӣ	[gurbai obiː]
dolphin	делфин	[delfin]

bear	хирс	[xirs]
polar bear	хирси сафед	[xirsi safed]
panda	панда	[panda]

monkey	маймун	[majmun]
chimpanzee	шимпанзе	[ʃimpanze]
orangutan	орангутанг	[orangutang]
gorilla	горилла	[gorilla]
macaque	макака	[makaka]
gibbon	гиббон	[gibbon]

| elephant | фил | [fil] |
| rhinoceros | карк, каркадан | [kark], [karkadan] |

| giraffe | заррофа | [zarrofa] |
| hippopotamus | баҳмут | [bahmut] |

| kangaroo | кенгуру | [kenguru] |
| koala (bear) | коала | [koala] |

mongoose	росу	[rosu]
chinchilla	вашақ	[vaʃaq]
skunk	скунс	[skuns]
porcupine	чайра, дугпушт	[dʒajra], [dugpuʃt]

89. Domestic animals

cat	гурба	[gurba]
tomcat	гурбаи нар	[gurbai nar]
dog	саг	[sag]

horse	асп	[asp]
stallion (male horse)	айғир, аспи нар	[ajʁir], [aspi nar]
mare	модиён, байтал	[modijɔn], [bajtal]

cow	гов	[gov]
bull	барзагов	[barzagov]
ox	барзагов	[barzagov]

sheep (ewe)	меш, гӯсфанд	[meʃ], [gœsfand]
ram	гӯсфанд	[gœsfand]
goat	буз	[buz]
billy goat, he-goat	така, серка	[taka], [serka]

donkey	хар, маркаб	[χar], [markab]
mule	хачир	[χatʃir]

pig, hog	хук	[χuq]
piglet	хукбача	[χukbatʃa]
rabbit	харгӯш	[χargœʃ]

hen (chicken)	мурғ	[murʁ]
rooster	хурӯс	[χurœs]

duck	мурғобӣ	[murʁobi:]
drake	мурғобии нар	[murʁobi:i nar]
goose	қоз, ғоз	[qoz], [ʁoz]

tom turkey, gobbler	хурӯси мурғи марҷон	[χurœsi murʁi mardʒon]
turkey (hen)	мокиёни мурғи марҷон	[mokijɔni murʁi mardʒon]

domestic animals	ҳайвони хонагӣ	[hajvoni χonagi:]
tame (e.g., ~ hamster)	ромшуда	[romʃuda]
to tame (vt)	дастомӯз кардан	[dastomœz kardan]
to breed (vt)	калон кардан	[kalon kardan]

farm	ферма	[ferma]
poultry	паррандаи хонагӣ	[parrandai χonagi:]
cattle	чорво	[tʃorvo]
herd (cattle)	пода	[poda]

stable	саисхона, аспхона	[saisχona], [aspχona]
pigpen	хукхона	[χukχona]
cowshed	оғил, говхона	[oʁil], [govχona]
rabbit hutch	харгӯшхона	[χargœʃχona]
hen house	мурғхона	[murʁχona]

90. Birds

bird	паранда	[paranda]
pigeon	кафтар	[kaftar]
sparrow	гунчишк, чумчук	[gundʒiʃk], [ʧumʧuk]
tit (great tit)	фотимачумчуқ	[fotimaʧumʧuq]
magpie	акка	[akka]
raven	зоғ	[zoʁ]
crow	зоғи ало	[zoʁi alo]
jackdaw	зоғча	[zoʁʧa]
rook	шӯрнӯл	[ʃœrnœl]
duck	мурғобӣ	[murʁobi:]
goose	қоз, ғоз	[qoz], [ʁoz]
pheasant	тазарв	[tazarv]
eagle	укоб	[ukob]
hawk	пайғу	[pajʁu]
falcon	боз, шоҳин	[boz], [ʃohin]
vulture	каргас	[kargas]
condor (Andean ~)	кондор	[kondor]
swan	қу	[qu]
crane	куланг, турна	[kulang], [turna]
stork	лаклак	[laklak]
parrot	тӯтӣ	[tœti:]
hummingbird	колибри	[kolibri]
peacock	товус	[tovus]
ostrich	шутурмурғ	[ʃuturmurʁ]
heron	ҳавосил	[havosil]
flamingo	бутимор	[butimor]
pelican	мурғи саққо	[murʁi saqqo]
nightingale	булбул	[bulbul]
swallow	фароштурук	[faroʃturuk]
thrush	дурроҷ	[durrodʒ]
song thrush	дуррочи хушхон	[durrodʒi xuʃxon]
blackbird	дуррочи сиёҳ	[durrodʒi sijoh]
swift	досак	[dosak]
lark	чӯр, чаковак	[dʒœr], [ʧakovak]
quail	бедона	[bedona]
cuckoo	фохтак	[foxtak]
owl	бум, чуғз	[bum], [dʒuʁz]
eagle owl	чуғз	[ʧuʁz]
wood grouse	дурроҷ	[durrodʒ]

| black grouse | титав | [titav] |
| partridge | кабк, каклик | [kabk], [kaklik] |

starling	сор, соч	[sor], [soʧ]
canary	канарейка	[kanarejka]
hazel grouse	рябчик	[rjabtʃik]
chaffinch	саъва	[sa'va]
bullfinch	севғар	[sevʁar]

seagull	моҳихӯрак	[mohiχœrak]
albatross	уқоби баҳрӣ	[uqobi bahri:]
penguin	пингвин	[pingvin]

91. Fish. Marine animals

bream	симмоҳӣ	[simmohi:]
carp	капур	[kapur]
perch	аломоҳӣ	[alomohi:]
catfish	лаққамоҳӣ	[laqqamohi:]
pike	шӯртан	[ʃœrtan]

| salmon | озодмоҳӣ | [ozodmohi:] |
| sturgeon | тосмоҳӣ | [tosmohi:] |

herring	шӯрмоҳӣ	[ʃœrmohi:]
Atlantic salmon	озодмоҳӣ	[ozodmoχi:]
mackerel	зағӯтамоҳӣ	[zaʁœtamohi:]
flatfish	камбала	[kambala]

zander, pike perch	суфмоҳӣ	[sufmohi:]
cod	равғанмоҳӣ	[ravʁanmohi:]
tuna	самак	[samak]
trout	гулмоҳӣ	[gulmohi:]

eel	мормоҳӣ	[mormohi:]
electric ray	скати барқдор	[skati barqdor]
moray eel	мурена	[murena]
piranha	пираня	[piranja]

shark	наҳанг	[nahang]
dolphin	делфин	[delfin]
whale	кит, наҳанг	[kit], [nahang]

crab	харчанг	[χarʧang]
jellyfish	медуза	[meduza]
octopus	ҳаштпо	[haʃtpo]

starfish	ситораи баҳрӣ	[sitorai bahri:]
sea urchin	хорпушти баҳрӣ	[χorpuʃti bahri:]
seahorse	аспакмоҳӣ	[aspakmohi:]

oyster	садафак	[sadafak]
shrimp	креветка	[krevetka]
lobster	харчанги баҳрӣ	[χartʃangi bahri:]
spiny lobster	лангуст	[langust]

92. Amphibians. Reptiles

| snake | мор | [mor] |
| venomous (snake) | заҳрдор | [zahrdor] |

viper	мори афъӣ	[mori afʼi:]
cobra	мори айнакдор, кӯбро	[mori ajnakdor], [kœbro]
python	мори печон	[mori petʃon]
boa	мори печон	[mori petʃon]

grass snake	мори обӣ	[mori obi:]
rattle snake	шақшақамор	[ʃaqʃaqamor]
anaconda	анаконда	[anakonda]

lizard	калтакалос	[kaltakalos]
iguana	сусмор, игуана	[susmor], [iguana]
monitor lizard	сусмор	[susmor]
salamander	калтакалос	[kaltakalos]
chameleon	бӯқаламун	[bœqalamun]
scorpion	каждум	[kaʒdum]

turtle	сангпушт	[sangpuʃt]
frog	қурбоққа	[qurboqqa]
toad	ғук, қурбоққаи чӯлӣ	[ʁuk], [qurboqqai tʃœli:]
crocodile	тимсоҳ	[timsoh]

93. Insects

insect, bug	ҳашарот	[haʃarot]
butterfly	шапалак	[ʃapalak]
ant	мӯрча	[mœrtʃa]
fly	магас	[magas]
mosquito	пашша	[paʃʃa]
beetle	гамбуск	[gambusk]

wasp	ору	[oru]
bee	занбӯри асал	[zanbœri asal]
bumblebee	говзанбӯр	[govzanbœr]
gadfly (botfly)	ғурмагас	[ʁurmagas]

spider	тортанак	[tortanak]
spiderweb	тори тортанак	[tori tortanak]
dragonfly	сӯзанак	[sœzanak]

| grasshopper | малах | [malaχ] |
| moth (night butterfly) | шапалак | [ʃapalak] |

cockroach	нонхӯрак	[nonχœrak]
tick	кана	[kana]
flea	кайк	[kajk]
midge	пашша	[paʃʃa]

locust	малах	[malaχ]
snail	тӯкумшуллуқ	[tœkumʃulluq]
cricket	чирчирак	[tʃirtʃirak]
lightning bug	шабтоб	[ʃabtob]
ladybug	момохолак	[momoχolak]
cockchafer	гамбуски саврӣ	[gambuski savri:]

leech	шуллук	[ʃulluk]
caterpillar	кирм	[kirm]
earthworm	кирм	[kirm]
larva	кирм	[kirm]

FLORA

T&P Books Publishing

94. Trees

tree	дарахт	[daraχt]
deciduous (adj)	паҳнбарг	[pahnbarg]
coniferous (adj)	... и сӯзанбарг	[i sœzanbarg]
evergreen (adj)	ҳамешасабз	[hameʃasabz]
apple tree	дарахти себ	[daraχti seb]
pear tree	дарахти нок	[daraχti nok]
sweet cherry tree	дарахти гелос	[daraχti gelos]
sour cherry tree	дарахти олуболу	[daraχti olubolu]
plum tree	дарахти олу	[daraχti olu]
birch	тӯс	[tœs]
oak	булут	[bulut]
linden tree	зерфун	[zerfun]
aspen	сиёҳбед	[sijɔhbed]
maple	заранг	[zarang]
spruce	коч, ел	[kodʒ], [el]
pine	санавбар	[sanavbar]
larch	кочи баргрез	[kodʒi bargrez]
fir tree	пихта	[piχta]
cedar	дарахти чалгӯза	[daraχti dʒalʁœza]
poplar	сафедор	[safedor]
rowan	губайро	[ʁubajro]
willow	бед	[bed]
alder	роздор	[rozdor]
beech	бук, олаш	[buk], [olaʃ]
elm	дарахти ларг	[daraχti larg]
ash (tree)	шумтол	[ʃumtol]
chestnut	шохбулут	[ʃohbulut]
magnolia	магнолия	[magnolija]
palm tree	нахл	[naχl]
cypress	дарахти сарв	[daraχti sarv]
mangrove	дарахти анбаҳ	[daraχti anbah]
baobab	баобаб	[baobab]
eucalyptus	эвкалипт	[ɛvkalipt]
sequoia	секвойя	[sekvojja]

95. Shrubs

bush	бутта	[butta]
shrub	бутта	[butta]
grapevine	ток	[tok]
vineyard	токзор	[tokzor]
raspberry bush	тамашк	[tamaʃk]
blackcurrant bush	қоти сиёх	[qoti sijɔh]
redcurrant bush	коти сурх	[koti surχ]
gooseberry bush	бектошй	[bektoʃi:]
acacia	акатсия, ақоқиё	[akatsija], [aqoqijɔ]
barberry	буттаи зирк	[buttai zirk]
jasmine	ёсуман	[jɔsuman]
juniper	арча, ардач	[artʃa], [ardadʒ]
rosebush	буттаи гул	[buttai gul]
dog rose	хуч	[χutʃ]

96. Fruits. Berries

fruit	мева, самар	[meva], [samar]
fruits	меваҳо, самарҳо	[mevaho], [samarho]
apple	себ	[seb]
pear	мурӯд, нок	[murœd], [nok]
plum	олу	[olu]
strawberry (garden ~)	қулфинай	[qulfinaj]
sour cherry	олуболу	[olubolu]
sweet cherry	гелос	[gelos]
grape	ангур	[angur]
raspberry	тамашк	[tamaʃk]
blackcurrant	қоти сиёх	[qoti sijɔh]
redcurrant	коти сурх	[koti surχ]
gooseberry	бектошй	[bektoʃi:]
cranberry	клюква	[kljukva]
orange	афлесун, пӯртахол	[aflesun], [pœrtaχol]
mandarin	норанг	[norang]
pineapple	ананас	[ananas]
banana	банан	[banan]
date	хурмо	[χurmo]
lemon	лиму	[limu]
apricot	дарахти зардолу	[daraχti zardolu]

peach	шафтолу	[ʃaftolu]
kiwi	кивй	[kivi:]
grapefruit	норинч	[norindʒ]

berry	буттамева	[buttameva]
berries	буттамевахо	[buttamevaho]
cowberry	брусника	[brusnika]
wild strawberry	тути заминй	[tuti zamini:]
bilberry	черника	[tʃernika]

97. Flowers. Plants

| flower | гул | [gul] |
| bouquet (of flowers) | дастаи гул | [dastai gul] |

rose (flower)	гул, гули садбарг	[gul], [guli sadbarg]
tulip	лола	[lola]
carnation	гули мехак	[guli meχak]
gladiolus	гули ёкут	[guli jɔqut]

cornflower	тугмагул	[tugmagul]
harebell	гули момо	[guli momo]
dandelion	коку	[koqu]
camomile	бобуна	[bobuna]

aloe	уд, сабр, алоэ	[ud], [sabr], [aloɛ]
cactus	гули ханчарй	[guli χandʒari:]
rubber plant, ficus	тутанчир	[tutandʒir]

lily	савсан	[savsan]
geranium	анчибар	[andʒibar]
hyacinth	сунбул	[sunbul]

mimosa	нозгул	[nozgul]
narcissus	наргис	[nargis]
nasturtium	настаран	[nastaran]

orchid	сахлаб, сухлаб	[sahlab], [sœhlab]
peony	гули ашрафй	[guli aʃrafi:]
violet	бунафша	[bunafʃa]

pansy	бунафшаи фарангй	[bunafʃai farangi:]
forget-me-not	марзангуш	[marzangœʃ]
daisy	гули марворидак	[guli marvoridak]

poppy	кукнор	[kœknor]
hemp	бангдона, канаб	[bangdona], [kanab]
mint	пудина	[pudina]
lily of the valley	гули барфак	[guli barfak]
snowdrop	бойчечак	[bojtʃetʃak]

nettle	газна	[gazna]
sorrel	шилха	[ʃilχa]
water lily	нилуфари сафед	[nilufari safed]
fern	фарн	[farn]
lichen	гулсанг	[gulsang]

greenhouse (tropical ~)	гулхона	[gulχona]
lawn	чаман, сабзазор	[tʃaman], [sabzazor]
flowerbed	гулзор	[gulzor]

plant	растанй	[rastani:]
grass	алаф	[alaf]
blade of grass	хас	[χas]

leaf	барг	[barg]
petal	гулбарг	[gulbarg]
stem	поя	[poja]
tuber	бех, дона	[beχ], [dona]

young plant (shoot)	неш	[neʃ]
thorn	хор	[χor]

to blossom (vi)	гул кардан	[gul kardan]
to fade, to wither	пажмурда шудан	[paʒmurda ʃudan]
smell (odor)	бӯй	[bœj]
to cut (flowers)	буридан	[buridan]
to pick (a flower)	кандан	[kandan]

98. Cereals, grains

grain	дона, ғалла	[dona], [ʁalla]
cereal crops	растаниҳои ғалладона	[rastanihoi ʁalladona]
ear (of barley, etc.)	хӯша	[χœʃa]

wheat	гандум	[gandum]
rye	чавдор	[dʒavdor]
oats	хуртумон	[hurtumon]

millet	арзан	[arzan]
barley	чав	[dʒav]

corn	чуворимакка	[dʒuvorimakka]
rice	шолй, биринч	[ʃoli:], [birindʒ]
buckwheat	марчумак	[mardʒumak]

pea plant	нахӯд	[naχœd]
kidney bean	лӯбиё	[lœbijo]
soy	соя	[soja]
lentil	наск	[nask]
beans (pulse crops)	лӯбиё	[lœbijo]

COUNTRIES OF
THE WORLD

T&P Books Publishing

Afghanistan	Афғонистон	[afʁoniston]
Albania	Албания	[albanija]
Argentina	Аргентина	[argentina]
Armenia	Арманистон	[armaniston]
Australia	Австралия	[avstralija]
Austria	Австрия	[avstrija]
Azerbaijan	Озарбойҷон	[ozarbojdʒon]
The Bahamas	Ҷазираҳои Багам	[dʒazirahoi bagam]
Bangladesh	Бангладеш	[bangladeʃ]
Belarus	Беларус	[belarus]
Belgium	Белгия	[belgija]
Bolivia	Боливия	[bolivija]
Bosnia and Herzegovina	Босния ва Ҳерсеговина	[bosnija va hersegovina]
Brazil	Бразилия	[brazilija]
Bulgaria	Булғористон	[bulʁoriston]
Cambodia	Камбоҷа	[kambodʒa]
Canada	Канада	[kanada]
Chile	Чиле	[tʃile]
China	Чин	[tʃin]
Colombia	Колумбия	[kolumbija]
Croatia	Хорватия	[χorvatija]
Cuba	Куба	[kuba]
Cyprus	Кипр	[kipr]
Czech Republic	Чехия	[tʃeχija]
Denmark	Дания	[danija]
Dominican Republic	Ҷумхурии Доминикан	[dʒumhuriːi dominikan]
Ecuador	Эквадор	[ɛkvador]
Egypt	Миср	[misr]
England	Англия	[anglija]
Estonia	Эстония	[ɛstonija]
Finland	Финланд	[finland]
France	Фаронса	[faronsa]
French Polynesia	Полинезияи Фаронсавӣ	[polinezijai faronsaviː]
Georgia	Гурҷистон	[gurdʒiston]
Germany	Олмон	[olmon]
Ghana	Гана	[gana]
Great Britain	Инглистон	[ingliston]
Greece	Юнон	[junon]
Haiti	Гаити	[gaiti]
Hungary	Маҷористон	[madʒoriston]

100. Countries. Part 2

Iceland	Исландия	[islandija]
India	Ҳиндустон	[hinduston]
Indonesia	Индонезия	[indonezija]
Iran	Эрон	[ɛron]
Iraq	Ироқ	[iroq]
Ireland	Ирландия	[irlandija]
Israel	Исроил	[isroil]
Italy	Итолиё	[itolijo]

Jamaica	Ямайка	[jamajka]
Japan	Жопун, Ҷопон	[ʒopun], [dʒopon]
Jordan	Урдун	[urdun]
Kazakhstan	Қазоқистон	[qazoqiston]
Kenya	Кения	[kenija]
Kirghizia	Қиргизистон	[qirʁiziston]
Kuwait	Кувайт	[kuvajt]
Laos	Лаос	[laos]
Latvia	Латвия	[latvija]
Lebanon	Лубнон	[lubnon]
Libya	Либия	[libija]
Liechtenstein	Лихтенштейн	[liχtenʃtejn]
Lithuania	Литва	[litva]
Luxembourg	Люксембург	[ljuksemburg]

Macedonia (Republic of ~)	Мақдуния	[maqdunija]
Madagascar	Мадагаскар	[madagaskar]
Malaysia	Малайзия	[malajzija]
Malta	Малта	[malta]
Mexico	Мексика	[meksika]
Moldova, Moldavia	Молдова	[moldova]

Monaco	Монако	[monako]
Mongolia	Муғулистон	[muʁuliston]
Montenegro	Монтенегро	[montenegro]
Morocco	Марокаш	[marokaʃ]
Myanmar	Мянма	[mjanma]
Namibia	Намибия	[namibija]
Nepal	Непал	[nepal]
Netherlands	Ҳоланд	[holand]
New Zealand	Зеландияи Нав	[zelandijai nav]
North Korea	Кореяи Шимолӣ	[korejai ʃimoli:]
Norway	Норвегия	[norvegija]

101. Countries. Part 3

| Pakistan | Покистон | [pokiston] |
| Palestine | Фаластин | [falastin] |

Panama	Панама	[panama]
Paraguay	Парагвай	[paragvaj]
Peru	Перу	[peru]
Poland	Полша, Лаҳистон	[polʃa], [lahiston]
Portugal	Португалия	[portugalija]
Romania	Руминия	[ruminija]
Russia	Россия	[rossija]

Saudi Arabia	Арабистони Саудй	[arabistoni saudi:]
Scotland	Шотландия	[ʃotlandija]
Senegal	Сенегал	[senegal]
Serbia	Сербия	[serbija]
Slovakia	Словакия	[slovakija]
Slovenia	Словения	[slovenija]

South Africa	Африқои Ҷанубй	[afriqoi dʒanubi:]
South Korea	Кореяи Ҷанубй	[korejai dʒanubi:]
Spain	Испониё	[isponijɔ]
Suriname	Суринам	[surinam]
Sweden	Шветсия	[ʃvetsija]
Switzerland	Швейсария	[ʃvejsarija]
Syria	Сурия	[surija]

Taiwan	Тайван	[tajvan]
Tajikistan	Тоҷикистон	[todʒikiston]
Tanzania	Танзания	[tanzanija]
Tasmania	Тасмания	[tasmanija]
Thailand	Таиланд	[tailand]
Tunisia	Тунис	[tunis]
Turkey	Туркия	[turkija]
Turkmenistan	Туркманистон	[turkmaniston]

Ukraine	Украйина	[ukrajina]
United Arab Emirates	Иморатҳои Муттаҳидаи Араб	[imorathoi muttahidai arab]
United States of America	Иёлоти Муттаҳидаи Америка	[ijɔloti muttahidai amerika]
Uruguay	Уругвай	[urugvaj]
Uzbekistan	Ӯзбакистон	[œzbakiston]

Vatican	Вотикон	[votikon]
Venezuela	Венесуэла	[venesuɛla]
Vietnam	Ветнам	[vetnam]
Zanzibar	Занзибар	[zanzibar]

GASTRONOMIC GLOSSARY

This section contains a lot of
words and terms associated
with food. This dictionary will
make it easier for you to
understand the menu at a
restaurant and choose
the right dish

T&P Books Publishing

English-Tajik gastronomic glossary

aftertaste	таъм	[ta'm]
almond	бодом	[bodom]
anise	тухми бодиён	[tuχmi bodijɔn]
aperitif	аперитив	[aperitiv]
appetite	иштихо	[iʃtiho]
appetizer	хӯриш, газак	[χœriʃ], [gazak]
apple	себ	[seb]
apricot	дарахти зардолу	[daraχti zardolu]
artichoke	анганор	[anganor]
asparagus	морчӯба	[mortʃœba]
Atlantic salmon	озодмохӣ	[ozodmoχi:]
avocado	авокадо	[avokado]
bacon	бекон	[bekon]
banana	банан	[banan]
barley	ҷав	[ʤav]
bartender	бармен	[barmen]
basil	нозбӯй, райхон	[nozbœj], [rajhon]
bay leaf	барги ғор	[bargi ʁor]
beans	лӯбиё	[lœbijo]
beef	гӯшти гов	[gœʃti gov]
beer	пиво	[pivo]
beetroot	лаблабу	[lablabu]
bell pepper	қаламфур	[qalamfur]
berries	буттамевахо	[buttamevaho]
berry	буттамева	[buttameva]
bilberry	черника	[tʃernika]
birch bolete	занбӯруғи тӯсӣ	[zanbœruʁi tœsi:]
bitter	талх	[talχ]
black coffee	қахваи сиёх	[qahvai sijɔh]
black pepper	мурчи сиёх	[murtʃi sijɔh]
black tea	чойи сиёх	[tʃoji sijɔh]
blackberry	марминчон	[marminʤon]
blackcurrant	қоти сиёх	[qoti sijɔh]
boiled	ҷӯшондашуда	[ʤœʃondaʃuda]
bottle opener	саркушояк	[sarkuʃojak]
bread	нон	[non]
breakfast	ноништа	[noniʃta]
bream	симмохӣ	[simmohi:]
broccoli	карами брокколӣ	[karami brokkoli:]
Brussels sprouts	карами брусселӣ	[karami brusseli:]
buckwheat	марчумак	[marʤumak]
butter	равгани маска	[ravʁani maska]
buttercream	крем	[krem]
cabbage	карам	[karam]

cake	пирожни	[piroʒni]
cake	торт	[tort]
calorie	калория	[kalorija]
can opener	саркушояк	[sarkuʃojak]
candy	конфет	[konfet]
canned food	консерв	[konserv]
cappuccino	капучино	[kaputʃino]
caraway	зира	[zira]
carbohydrates	карбогидратхо	[karbogidratho]
carbonated	газнок	[gaznok]
carp	капур	[kapur]
carrot	сабзӣ	[sabzi:]
catfish	лаққамохӣ	[laqqamohi:]
cauliflower	гулкарам	[gulkaram]
caviar	тухми мохӣ	[tuxmi mohi:]
celery	карафс	[karafs]
cep	занбӯруғи сафед	[zanbœruʁi safed]
cereal crops	растанихои ғалладона	[rastanihoi ʁalladona]
cereal grains	ярма	[jarma]
champagne	шампан	[ʃampan]
chanterelle	қӯзиқандӣ	[qœziqandi:]
check	хисоб	[hisob]
cheese	панир	[panir]
chewing gum	сақич, илқ	[saqitʃ], [ilq]
chicken	мурғ	[murʁ]
chocolate	шоколад	[ʃokolad]
chocolate	… и шоколад,	[i ʃokolad],
	шоколадӣ	[ʃokoladi:]
cinnamon	дорчин, долчин	[dortʃin], [doltʃin]
clear soup	булён	[buljɔn]
cloves	қаланфури гардан	[qalanfuri gardan]
cocktail	коктейл	[koktejl]
coconut	норгил	[norgil]
cod	равғанмохӣ	[ravʁanmohi:]
coffee	қахва	[qahva]
coffee with milk	ширқахва	[ʃirqahva]
cognac	коняк	[konjak]
cold	хунук	[xunuk]
condensed milk	ширқиём	[ʃirqijɔm]
condiment	хӯриш	[xœriʃ]
confectionery	махсулоти қанноди	[mahsuloti qannodi]
cookies	кулчақанд	[kultʃaqand]
coriander	кашнич	[kaʃnidʒ]
corkscrew	пӯккашак	[pœkkaʃak]
corn	чуворимакка	[dʒuvorimakka]
corn	чуворимакка	[dʒuvorimakka]
cornflakes	бадроқи чуворимакка	[badroqi dʒuvorimakka]
course, dish	таом	[taom]
cowberry	брусника	[brusnika]
crab	харчанг	[xartʃang]
cranberry	клюква	[kljukva]
cream	қаймоқ	[qajmoq]

crumb	резгӣ	[rezgi:]
crustaceans	буғумпойхо	[buʁumpojho]
cucumber	бодиринг	[bodiring]
cuisine	таомхо	[taomho]
cup	косача	[kosatʃa]
dark beer	оби чави торик	[obi dʒavi torik]
date	хурмо	[xurmo]
death cap	занбӯруғи захрнок	[zanbœruʁi zahrnok]
dessert	десерт	[desert]
diet	диета	[dieta]
dill	шибит	[ʃibit]
dinner	шом	[ʃom]
dried	хушк	[xuʃk]
drinking water	оби нӯшиданӣ	[obi nœʃidani:]
duck	мурғобӣ	[murʁobi:]
ear	хӯша	[xœʃa]
edible mushroom	занбӯруғи хӯрданӣ	[zanbœruʁi xœrdani:]
eel	мормохӣ	[mormohi:]
egg	тухм	[tuxm]
egg white	сафедии тухм	[safedi:i tuxm]
egg yolk	зардии тухм	[zardi:i tuxm]
eggplant	бодинчон	[bodindʒon]
eggs	тухм	[tuxm]
Enjoy your meal!	ош шавад!	[oʃ ʃavad]
fats	равған	[ravʁan]
fig	анчир	[andʒir]
filling	пур кардани, андохтани	[pur kardani], [andoxtani]
fish	мохӣ	[mohi:]
flatfish	камбала	[kambala]
flour	орд	[ord]
fly agaric	маргимагас	[margimagas]
food	хӯрок, таом	[xœrok], [taom]
fork	чангча, чангол	[tʃangtʃa], [tʃangol]
freshly squeezed juice	афшураи тоза тайёршуда	[afʃurai toza tajjorʃuda]
fried	бирён	[birjon]
fried eggs	тухмбирён	[tuxmbirjon]
frozen	яхкарда	[jaxkarda]
fruit	мева	[meva]
fruits	мевахо, самархо	[mevaho], [samarho]
game	сайди шикор	[sajdi ʃikor]
gammon	рон	[ron]
garlic	сир	[sir]
gin	чин	[dʒin]
ginger	занчабил	[zandʒabil]
glass	стакан	[stakan]
glass	бокал	[bokal]
goose	қоз, ғоз	[qoz], [ʁoz]
gooseberry	бектошӣ	[bektoʃi:]
grain	дона, ғалла	[dona], [ʁalla]
grape	ангур	[angur]
grapefruit	норинч	[norindʒ]

green tea	чои кабуд	[ʧoi kabud]
greens	сабзавот	[sabzavot]
halibut	палтус	[paltus]
ham	ветчина	[vetʧina]
hamburger	гӯшти кӯфта	[gœʃti kœfta]
hamburger	гамбургер	[gamburger]
hazelnut	финдиқ	[findiq]
herring	шӯрмоҳӣ	[ʃœrmohi:]
honey	асал	[asal]
horseradish	қаҳзак	[qahzak]
hot	гарм	[garm]
ice	ях	[jaχ]
ice-cream	яхмос	[jaχmos]
instant coffee	қаҳваи кӯфта	[qahvai kœfta]
jam	чем	[ʤem]
jam	мураббо	[murabbo]
juice	шарбат	[ʃarbat]
kidney bean	лӯбиё	[lœbijɔ]
kiwi	кивӣ	[kivi:]
knife	корд	[kord]
lamb	гӯшти гӯсфанд	[gœʃti gœsfand]
lemon	лиму	[limu]
lemonade	лимонад	[limonad]
lentil	наск	[nask]
lettuce	коху	[kohu]
light beer	оби ҷави шафоф	[obi ʤavi ʃafof]
liqueur	ликёр	[likjɔr]
liquors	нӯшокиҳои спиртӣ	[nœʃokihoi spirti:]
liver	ҷигар	[ʤigar]
lunch	хӯроки пешин	[χœroki peʃin]
mackerel	загӯтамоҳӣ	[zaʁœtamohi:]
mandarin	норанг	[norang]
mango	анбаҳ	[anbah]
margarine	маргарин	[margarin]
marmalade	мармалод	[marmalod]
mashed potatoes	пюре	[pjure]
mayonnaise	майонез	[majɔnez]
meat	гӯшт	[gœʃt]
menu	меню	[menju]
milk	шир	[ʃir]
milkshake	коктейли ширӣ	[koktejli ʃiri:]
millet	арзан	[arzan]
mineral water	оби минералӣ	[obi minerali:]
morel	бурмазанбӯруғ	[burmazanbœruʁ]
mushroom	занбӯруғ	[zanbœruʁ]
mustard	хардал	[χardal]
non-alcoholic	беалкогол	[bealkogol]
noodles	угро	[ugro]
oats	хуртумон	[hurtumon]
olive oil	равғани зайтун	[ravʁani zajtun]
olives	зайтун	[zajtun]
omelet	омлет, тухмбирён	[omlet], [tuχmbirjon]

onion	пиёз	[pijɔz]
orange	афлесун, пӯртахол	[aflesun], [pœrtaχol]
orange juice	афшураи афлесун	[aʃʃurai aflesun]
orange-cap boletus	занбӯруғи сурх	[zanbœruʁi surχ]
oyster	садафак	[sadafak]
pâté	паштет	[paʃtet]
papaya	папайя	[papajja]
paprika	қаламфур	[qalamfur]
parsley	чаъфарӣ	[dʒaʻfari:]
pasta	макарон	[makaron]
pea	нахӯд	[naχœd]
peach	шафтолу	[ʃaftolu]
peanut	финдуки заминӣ	[finduki zamini:]
pear	мурӯд, нок	[murœd], [nok]
peel	пӯст	[pœst]
perch	аломохӣ	[alomohi:]
pickled	дар сирко хобондашуда	[dar sirko χobondaʃuda]
pie	пирог	[pirog]
piece	порча	[porʧa]
pike	шӯртан	[ʃœrtan]
pike perch	суфмохӣ	[sufmohi:]
pineapple	ананас	[ananas]
pistachios	писта	[pista]
pizza	питса	[pitsa]
plate	тақсимча	[taqsimʧa]
plum	олу	[olu]
poisonous mushroom	занбӯруғи захрнок	[zanbœruʁi zahrnok]
pomegranate	анор	[anor]
pork	гӯшти хук	[gœʃti χuk]
porridge	шӯла	[ʃœla]
portion	навола	[navola]
potato	картошка	[kartoʃka]
proteins	сафедахо	[safedaho]
pub, bar	бар	[bar]
pudding	пудинг	[puding]
pumpkin	каду	[kadu]
rabbit	харгӯш	[χargœʃ]
radish	шалғамча	[ʃaʁamʧa]
raisin	мавиз	[maviz]
raspberry	тамашк	[tamaʃk]
recipe	ретсепт	[retsept]
red pepper	мурчи сурх	[murʧi surχ]
red wine	маи арғувонӣ	[mai arʁuvoni:]
redcurrant	коти сурх	[koti surχ]
refreshing drink	нӯшокии хунук	[nœʃoki:i χunuk]
rice	биринч	[birindʒ]
rum	ром	[rom]
russula	занбӯруғи хомхӯрак	[zanbœruʁi χomχœrak]
rye	чавдор	[dʒavdor]
saffron	заъфарон	[zaʻfaron]
salad	салат	[salat]

salmon	озодмоҳӣ	[ozodmohi:]
salt	намак	[namak]
salty	шӯр	[ʃœr]
sandwich	бутерброд	[buterbrod]
sardine	саморис	[samoris]
sauce	қайла	[qajla]
saucer	тақсимӣ, тақсимича	[taqsimi:], [taqsimitʃa]
sausage	ҳасиб	[hasib]
seafood	маҳсулоти баҳрӣ	[mahsuloti bahri:]
sesame	кунҷид	[kundʒid]
shark	наҳанг	[nahang]
shrimp	креветка	[krevetka]
side dish	хӯриши таом	[xœriʃi taom]
slice	тилим, порча	[tilim], [portʃa]
smoked	дудхӯрда	[dudxœrda]
soft drink	нӯшокии беалкогол	[nœʃoki:i bealkogol]
soup	шӯрбо	[ʃœrbo]
soup spoon	қошуқи ошхӯрӣ	[qoʃuqi oʃxœri:]
sour cherry	олуболу	[olubolu]
sour cream	қаймоқ	[qajmok]
soy	соя	[soja]
spaghetti	спагеттӣ	[spagetti:]
sparkling	газдор	[gazdor]
spice	дорувор	[doruvor]
spinach	испаноқ	[ispanoq]
spiny lobster	лангуст	[langust]
spoon	қошуқ	[qoʃuq]
squid	калмар	[kalmar]
steak	бифштекс	[bifʃteks]
still	бе газ	[be gaz]
strawberry	қулфинай	[qulfinaj]
sturgeon	гӯшти тосмоҳӣ	[gœʃti tosmohi:]
sugar	шакар	[ʃakar]
sunflower oil	равғани офтобпараст	[ravʁani oftobparast]
sweet	ширин	[ʃirin]
sweet cherry	гелос	[gelos]
taste, flavor	маза, таъм	[maza], [ta'm]
tasty	бомаза	[bomaza]
tea	чой	[tʃoj]
teaspoon	чойкошук	[tʃojkoʃuk]
tip	чойпулӣ	[tʃojpuli:]
tomato	помидор	[pomidor]
tomato juice	шираи помидор	[ʃirai pomidor]
tongue	забон	[zabon]
toothpick	дандонковак	[dandonkovak]
trout	гулмоҳӣ	[gulmohi:]
tuna	самак	[samak]
turkey	мурғи марҷон	[murʁi mardʒon]
turnip	шалғам	[ʃalʁam]
veal	гӯшти гӯсола	[gœʃti gœsola]
vegetable oil	равғани пок	[ravʁani pok]
vegetables	сабзавот	[sabzavot]

vegetarian	гӯштнахӯранда	[gœʃtnaxœranda]
vegetarian	бегӯшт	[begœʃt]
vermouth	вермут	[vermut]
vienna sausage	ҳасибча	[hasibtʃa]
vinegar	сирко	[sirko]
vitamin	витамин	[vitamin]
vodka	арақ, водка	[araq], [vodka]
waffles	вафлӣ	[vafli:]
waiter	пешхизмат	[peʃxizmat]
waitress	пешхизмат	[peʃxizmat]
walnut	чормағз	[tʃormaʁz]
water	об	[ob]
watermelon	тарбуз	[tarbuz]
wheat	гандум	[gandum]
whiskey	виски	[viski]
white wine	маи ангури сафед	[mai anguri safed]
wild strawberry	тути заминӣ	[tuti zamini:]
wine	шароб, май	[ʃarob], [maj]
wine list	рӯйхати шаробҳо	[rœjxati ʃarobho]
with ice	бо ях, яхдор	[bo jax], [jaxdor]
yogurt	йогурт	[jogurt]
zucchini	таррак	[tarrak]

кӯзиқандӣ	[qœziqandi:]	chanterelle
қаҳва	[qahva]	coffee
қаҳваи кӯфта	[qahvai kœfta]	instant coffee
қаҳваи сиёҳ	[qahvai sijɔh]	black coffee
қаҳзак	[qahzak]	horseradish
қайла	[qajla]	sauce
қаймоқ	[qajmoq]	cream
қаймок	[qajmok]	sour cream
қаламфур	[qalamfur]	bell pepper
қаламфур	[qalamfur]	paprika
қаланфури гардан	[qalanfuri gardan]	cloves
қоз, ғоз	[qoz], [ʁoz]	goose
қоти сиёҳ	[qoti sijɔh]	blackcurrant
қошуқ	[qoʃuq]	spoon
қошуқи ошхӯрӣ	[qoʃuqi oʃœri:]	soup spoon
қулфинай	[qulfinaj]	strawberry
ҳасиб	[hasib]	sausage
ҳасибча	[hasibtʃa]	vienna sausage
ҳисоб	[hisob]	check
ҳуртумон	[hurtumon]	oats
чӯшондашуда	[dʒœʃondaʃuda]	boiled
ҷав	[dʒav]	barley
ҷавдор	[dʒavdor]	rye
ҷаъфарӣ	[dʒa'fari:]	parsley
ҷем	[dʒem]	jam
ҷигар	[dʒigar]	liver
ҷин	[dʒin]	gin
ҷувworимакка	[dʒuvorimakka]	corn
ҷувориmакка	[dʒuvorimakka]	corn
авокадо	[avokado]	avocado
аломохӣ	[alomohi:]	perch
анҷир	[andʒir]	fig
ананас	[ananas]	pineapple
анбаҳ	[anbah]	mango
анганор	[anganor]	artichoke
ангур	[angur]	grape
анор	[anor]	pomegranate
аперитив	[aperitiv]	aperitif
арақ, водка	[araq], [vodka]	vodka
арзан	[arzan]	millet
асал	[asal]	honey
афлесун, пӯртахол	[aflesun], [pœrtaχol]	orange
афшураи тоза тайёршуда	[afʃurai toza tajjɔrʃuda]	freshly squeezed juice

афшураи афлесун	[afʃurai aflesun]	orange juice
бадроқи чуворимакка	[badroqi dʒuvorimakka]	cornflakes
банан	[banan]	banana
бар	[bar]	pub, bar
барги ғор	[bargi ʁor]	bay leaf
бармен	[barmen]	bartender
бе газ	[be gaz]	still
беалкогол	[bealkogol]	non-alcoholic
бегӯшт	[begœʃt]	vegetarian
бекон	[bekon]	bacon
бектошй	[bektoʃi:]	gooseberry
бирён	[birjon]	fried
биринч	[birindʒ]	rice
бифштекс	[bifʃteks]	steak
бо ях, яхдор	[bo jaχ], [jaχdor]	with ice
бодинчон	[bodindʒon]	eggplant
бодиринг	[bodiring]	cucumber
бодом	[bodom]	almond
бокал	[bokal]	glass
бомаза	[bomaza]	tasty
брусника	[brusnika]	cowberry
буғумпойхо	[buʁumpojho]	crustaceans
булён	[buljon]	clear soup
бурмазанбӯруғ	[burmazanbœruʁ]	morel
бутерброд	[buterbrod]	sandwich
буттамева	[buttameva]	berry
буттамевахо	[buttamevaho]	berries
вафлй	[vafli:]	waffles
вермут	[vermut]	vermouth
ветчина	[vettʃina]	ham
виски	[viski]	whiskey
витамин	[vitamin]	vitamin
гӯшт	[gœʃt]	meat
гӯшти гӯсола	[gœʃti gœsola]	veal
гӯшти гӯсфанд	[gœʃti gœsfand]	lamb
гӯшти гов	[gœʃti gov]	beef
гӯшти кӯфта	[gœʃti kœfta]	hamburger
гӯшти тосмохй	[gœʃti tosmohi:]	sturgeon
гӯшти хук	[gœʃti χuk]	pork
гӯштнахӯранда	[gœʃtnaχœranda]	vegetarian
газдор	[gazdor]	sparkling
газнок	[gaznok]	carbonated
гамбургер	[gamburger]	hamburger
гандум	[gandum]	wheat
гарм	[garm]	hot
гелос	[gelos]	sweet cherry
гулкарам	[gulkaram]	cauliflower
гулмохй	[gulmohi:]	trout
дандонковак	[dandonkovak]	toothpick
дар сирко хобондашуда	[dar sirko χobondaʃuda]	pickled
дарахти зардолу	[daraχti zardolu]	apricot

десерт	[desert]	dessert
диета	[dieta]	diet
дона, ғалла	[dona], [ʁalla]	grain
дорувор	[doruvor]	spice
дорчин, долчин	[dortʃin], [doltʃin]	cinnamon
дудхӯрда	[dudχœrda]	smoked
зағӯтамоҳӣ	[zaʁœtamohi:]	mackerel
забон	[zabon]	tongue
зайтун	[zajtun]	olives
занҷабил	[zandʒabil]	ginger
занбӯруғ	[zanbœruʁ]	mushroom
занбӯруғи заҳрнок	[zanbœruʁi zahrnok]	poisonous mushroom
занбӯруғи заҳрнок	[zanbœruʁi zahrnok]	death cap
занбӯруғи сафед	[zanbœruʁi safed]	cep
занбӯруғи сурх	[zanbœruʁi surχ]	orange-cap boletus
занбӯруғи тӯсӣ	[zanbœruʁi tœsi:]	birch bolete
занбӯруғи хӯрданӣ	[zanbœruʁi χœrdani:]	edible mushroom
занбӯруғи хомхӯрак	[zanbœruʁi χomχœrak]	russula
зардии тухм	[zardi:i tuχm]	egg yolk
заъфарон	[za'faron]	saffron
зира	[zira]	caraway
испаноқ	[ispanoq]	spinach
иштиҳо	[iʃtiho]	appetite
йогурт	[jɔgurt]	yogurt
каду	[kadu]	pumpkin
калмар	[kalmar]	squid
калория	[kalorija]	calorie
камбала	[kambala]	flatfish
капур	[kapur]	carp
капучино	[kaputʃino]	cappuccino
карам	[karam]	cabbage
карами брокколӣ	[karami brokkoli:]	broccoli
карами брусселӣ	[karami brusseli:]	Brussels sprouts
карафс	[karafs]	celery
карбогидратҳо	[karbogidratho]	carbohydrates
картошка	[kartoʃka]	potato
кашнич	[kaʃnidʒ]	coriander
кивӣ	[kivi:]	kiwi
клюква	[kljukva]	cranberry
коҳу	[kohu]	lettuce
коктейл	[koktejl]	cocktail
коктейли ширӣ	[koktejli ʃiri:]	milkshake
консерв	[konserv]	canned food
конфет	[konfet]	candy
коняк	[konjak]	cognac
корд	[kord]	knife
косача	[kosatʃa]	cup
коти сурх	[koti surχ]	redcurrant
креветка	[krevetka]	shrimp
крем	[krem]	buttercream
кулчақанд	[kultʃaqand]	cookies
кунҷид	[kundʒid]	sesame

лӯбиё	[lœbijɔ]	beans
лӯбиё	[lœbijɔ]	kidney bean
лаққамохӣ	[laqqamohi:]	catfish
лаблабу	[lablabu]	beetroot
лангуст	[langust]	spiny lobster
ликёр	[likjɔr]	liqueur
лимонад	[limonad]	lemonade
лиму	[limu]	lemon
маҳсулоти қанноди	[mahsuloti qannodi]	confectionery
маҳсулоти баҳрӣ	[mahsuloti bahri:]	seafood
мавиз	[maviz]	raisin
маза, таъм	[maza], [ta'm]	taste, flavor
маи ангури сафед	[mai anguri safed]	white wine
маи арғувонӣ	[mai arʁuvoni:]	red wine
майонез	[majɔnez]	mayonnaise
макарон	[makaron]	pasta
марчумак	[mardʒumak]	buckwheat
маргарин	[margarin]	margarine
маргимагас	[margimagas]	fly agaric
мармалод	[marmalod]	marmalade
марминчон	[marmindʒon]	blackberry
мева	[meva]	fruit
меваҳо, самарҳо	[mevaho], [samarho]	fruits
меню	[menju]	menu
моҳӣ	[mohi:]	fish
мормоҳӣ	[mormohi:]	eel
морчӯба	[mortʃœba]	asparagus
мурғ	[murʁ]	chicken
мурғи марчон	[murʁi mardʒon]	turkey
мурғобӣ	[murʁobi:]	duck
мурӯд, нок	[murœd], [nok]	pear
мураббо	[murabbo]	jam
мурчи сиёҳ	[murtʃi sijɔh]	black pepper
мурчи сурх	[murtʃi surχ]	red pepper
нӯшокиҳои спиртӣ	[nœʃokihoi spirti:]	liquors
нӯшокии беалкогол	[nœʃoki:i bealkogol]	soft drink
нӯшокии хунук	[nœʃoki:i χunuk]	refreshing drink
наҳанг	[nahang]	shark
навола	[navola]	portion
намак	[namak]	salt
наск	[nask]	lentil
нахӯд	[naχœd]	pea
нозбӯй, райҳон	[nozbœj], [rajhon]	basil
нон	[non]	bread
ношишта	[noniʃta]	breakfast
норанг	[norang]	mandarin
норгил	[norgil]	coconut
норинч	[norindʒ]	grapefruit
об	[ob]	water
оби чави торик	[obi dʒavi torik]	dark beer
оби чави шафоф	[obi dʒavi ʃafof]	light beer
оби минералӣ	[obi minerali:]	mineral water

оби нӯшиданӣ	[obi nœʃidani:]	drinking water
озодмоҳӣ	[ozodmohi:]	salmon
озодмохӣ	[ozodmoχi:]	Atlantic salmon
олу	[olu]	plum
олуболу	[olubolu]	sour cherry
омлет, тухмбирён	[omlet], [tuχmbirjɔn]	omelet
орд	[ord]	flour
ош шавад!	[oʃ ʃavad]	Enjoy your meal!
пӯккашак	[pœkkaʃak]	corkscrew
пӯст	[pœst]	peel
палтус	[paltus]	halibut
панир	[panir]	cheese
папайя	[papajja]	papaya
паштет	[paʃtet]	pâté
пешхизмат	[peʃχizmat]	waiter
пешхизмат	[peʃχizmat]	waitress
пиво	[pivo]	beer
пиёз	[pijɔz]	onion
пирог	[pirog]	pie
пирожни	[pirɔʒni]	cake
писта	[pista]	pistachios
питса	[pitsa]	pizza
помидор	[pomidor]	tomato
порча	[portʃa]	piece
пудинг	[puding]	pudding
пур кардани, андохтани	[pur kardani], [andoχtani]	filling
пюре	[pjure]	mashed potatoes
рӯйхати шаробҳо	[rœjχati ʃarobho]	wine list
равған	[ravʁan]	fats
равғани зайтун	[ravʁani zajtun]	olive oil
равғани маска	[ravʁani maska]	butter
равғани офтобпараст	[ravʁani oftobparast]	sunflower oil
равғани пок	[ravʁani pok]	vegetable oil
равғанмоҳӣ	[ravʁanmohi:]	cod
растаниҳои ғалладона	[rastanihoi ʁalladona]	cereal crops
резгӣ	[rezgi:]	crumb
ретсепт	[retsept]	recipe
ром	[rom]	rum
рон	[ron]	gammon
сақич, илқ	[saqitʃ], [ilq]	chewing gum
сабзӣ	[sabzi:]	carrot
сабзавот	[sabzavot]	vegetables
сабзавот	[sabzavot]	greens
садафак	[sadafak]	oyster
сайди шикор	[sajdi ʃikor]	game
салат	[salat]	salad
самак	[samak]	tuna
саморис	[samoris]	sardine
саркушояк	[sarkuʃojak]	bottle opener
саркушояк	[sarkuʃojak]	can opener
сафедаҳо	[safedaho]	proteins
сафедии тухм	[safedi:i tuχm]	egg white

себ	[seb]	apple
симмоҳӣ	[simmohi:]	bream
сир	[sir]	garlic
сирко	[sirko]	vinegar
соя	[soja]	soy
спагеттӣ	[spagetti:]	spaghetti
стакан	[stakan]	glass
суфмоҳӣ	[sufmohi:]	pike perch
тақсимӣ, тақсимича	[taqsimi:], [taqsimitʃa]	saucer
тақсимча	[taqsimtʃa]	plate
талх	[talχ]	bitter
тамашк	[tamaʃk]	raspberry
таом	[taom]	course, dish
таомҳо	[taomho]	cuisine
тарбуз	[tarbuz]	watermelon
таррак	[tarrak]	zucchini
таъм	[ta'm]	aftertaste
тилим, порча	[tilim], [portʃa]	slice
торт	[tort]	cake
тути заминӣ	[tuti zamini:]	wild strawberry
тухм	[tuχm]	egg
тухм	[tuχm]	eggs
тухмбирён	[tuχmbirjɔn]	fried eggs
тухми бодиён	[tuχmi bodijɔn]	anise
тухми моҳӣ	[tuχmi mohi:]	caviar
угро	[ugro]	noodles
финдиқ	[findiq]	hazelnut
финдуки заминӣ	[finduki zamini:]	peanut
хӯриш	[χœriʃ]	condiment
хӯриш, газак	[χœriʃ], [gazak]	appetizer
хӯриши таом	[χœriʃi taom]	side dish
хӯрок, таом	[χœrok], [taom]	food
хӯроки пешин	[χœroki peʃin]	lunch
хӯша	[χœʃa]	ear
харгӯш	[χargœʃ]	rabbit
хардал	[χardal]	mustard
харчанг	[χartʃang]	crab
хунук	[χunuk]	cold
хурмо	[χurmo]	date
хушк	[χuʃk]	dried
чангча, чангол	[tʃangtʃa], [tʃangol]	fork
черника	[tʃernika]	bilberry
чои кабуд	[tʃoi kabud]	green tea
чой	[tʃoj]	tea
чойи сиёҳ	[tʃoji sijɔh]	black tea
чойкошук	[tʃojkoʃuk]	teaspoon
чойпулӣ	[tʃojpuli:]	tip
чормағз	[tʃormaʁz]	walnut
шӯла	[ʃœla]	porridge
шӯр	[ʃœr]	salty
шӯрбо	[ʃœrbo]	soup
шӯрмоҳӣ	[ʃœrmohi:]	herring

шӯртан	[ʃœrtan]	pike
шакар	[ʃakar]	sugar
шалғам	[ʃalʁam]	turnip
шалғамча	[ʃalʁamtʃa]	radish
шампан	[ʃampan]	champagne
шарбат	[ʃarbat]	juice
шароб, май	[ʃarob], [maj]	wine
шафтолу	[ʃaftolu]	peach
шибит	[ʃibit]	dill
шир	[ʃir]	milk
ширқаҳва	[ʃirqahva]	coffee with milk
ширқиём	[ʃirqijɔm]	condensed milk
шираи помидор	[ʃirai pomidor]	tomato juice
ширин	[ʃirin]	sweet
шоколад	[ʃokolad]	chocolate
шом	[ʃom]	dinner
ярма	[jarma]	cereal grains
ях	[jaχ]	ice
яхкарда	[jaχkarda]	frozen
яхмос	[jaχmos]	ice-cream
... и шоколад, шоколадй	[i ʃokolad], [ʃokoladi:]	chocolate

Made in the USA
Middletown, DE
02 May 2022

65107614R00117